MW01004101

THE JESUS I KNOW

Robert K Wolthuis

Published by Ringmasters Media
2437 N Rulon White Blvd.
Ogden UT 84404

Cover design by Misty Choate

Picture credits: David Bowman - *Innocence.* Used with permission.

Edited by: Heather Godfrey.
Layout by: Kirk Edwards

ISBN: 978-1-942298-13-7

CONTENTS

PREFACE

When I began to seriously study and ponder the life of Jesus Christ, I found that most non-scripture accounts focused on the details of His life and mission as the Messiah and Savior of the world as found in the New Testament. I accept without question that He is the Son of God, was the major architect and builder of the earth, and came here as the Only Begotten of God the Father to be the Savior of all mankind. However, few commentators have tried to capture the essence of Jesus as a man whom people could know and relate to as a warm, caring friend. These observations led me to carefully investigate the life of Christ and to write this small treatise describing the Jesus I know.

For nearly 30 years I served in the US Government where I had the privilege of observing and working for a lot of powerful and famous individuals including Presidents, Cabinet members, Senators, Congressmen and senior military officers. Within my Federal Service and various callings in the LDS Church, I have been able to watch how human beings treat each other. I pondered on the real nature of humanity, and often wondered as I worked with victims of natural and manmade disasters, how would the Savior handle such situations? If He were suddenly in the presence of an American President, a rich and famous celebrity, and a poor urchin from a city slum, what protocol would Christ follow? As a result of my life's experiences, considerate study of the scriptures, and distinct impressions, I think He would embrace the urchin first.

My purpose in writing this book is to demonstrate that this Man loved and served the poor, the humble, and the common people as an integral part of His mortal ministry. As proof of Christ's love for all mankind, I have documented Christ's relationship with several people, ranging from the great apostle Peter to some of the most unfortunate people in all of Israel, the lepers, those who could not walk, and some who were blind. He healed them, he forgave them, and He loved them. To these people He was Savior, healing physician, and dear friend.

Each individual has to answer the eternal questions concerning the existence of God, the Messiahship of Jesus Christ, and what role each one will play in his or her life. Fortunately or unfortunately, these critical issues cannot be resolved in the laboratory or through the scientific process. It comes from faith and trust in God and a protocol of believing prayer.

It is not my role or purpose, nor do I have the capacity, to pass onto anyone my convictions, feelings, and interpretation of the meaning and life of Jesus Christ. All I can do is record them here; the reader will be the sole judge as to their value in his or her life. The views I present here are my own and my sole responsibility. I do not purport to represent them as doctrines and beliefs of The Church of Jesus Christ of Latter-day Saints of which I am a devout member. Much of the basic data is taken from recorded scripture. The interpretation and meaning placed thereon are my own personal views.

Chapter One

A Brief Sketch of the Jesus I Know

Each person professing the Christian faith has a perception or image of Jesus Christ. As part of that exercise of our religious faith, I am certain that many Christians sometimes ask, "What would Christ do?" or "How would the Savior see what I see, or experience what I am experiencing?" I have taken the liberty of noting here my views of how Christ would see selected things in human relations and the physical world in which we live.

The Jesus I know is a warm, kind, friendly, tough, gentle and wonderful man. I even believe He has a sense of humor although it is seldom, if ever, recorded in scripture and most writings. He has, in my view, all the wonderful characteristics we attribute to cherished grandparents, dads, moms, brothers, sisters, church leaders, dear friends, and worthy heroes.

The Jesus I know would love fishing, horseback riding, gardening, Secretariat's win in the 1973 Belmont, and a thoughtful sermon ended on time. He appreciates small acts of kindness, tears at a close friend's funeral, and respects the scientific accomplishments of the Space Shuttle, modern electronics, and an MRI, all of which are very primitive by His standards of knowledge and accomplishment. Jesus would enjoy viewing the Grand Canyon, the majesty of Alaska, the Swiss Alps, and the steppes of Russia. The Savior would be touched by Schubert's

"Serenade," the haunting melody of "Ashokan Farewell", and a stirring rendition of "How Great Thou Art." I feel He would be amused at the futility of most legislative and parliamentary bodies, saddened by the abject poverty of the world's poor, touched by a young boy's first violin recital, and a sweet five-year-old girl's first ballet lesson. He is, I believe, deeply saddened and angered when an unnecessary abortion is performed or a child is abused or murdered.

I believe He is repulsed at the amount of money paid to professional athletes, entertainers, and business executives while so many of His brothers and sisters in the world are homeless and hungry. He is respectful of the American corn crop and the wheat harvest in the Ukraine, sickened by the behavior of some prominent political figures, the tobacco companies and deceptive advertising. Christ is undoubtedly touched by the first steps of a ten-month old toddler and pleased when a fourteen-year-old boy refuses to use drugs.

Having given His life for others, He is respectful of the brave men who died on the beaches of Normandy, at Stalingrad and Gettysburg. He is saddened and mindful of His Father's noble sons and daughters who died at Auschwitz, in the Gulag Archipelago, and in the Asian prison camps. I believe Jesus appreciates the works of the great masters of art, music, and literature, and the proud efforts of a three-year-old's first picture scribbled in crayon on his bedroom wall. He welcomes with open arms a young mother whose life is ended by disease or at childbirth, and a venerable elder from the interior of China or the mountains of Bolivia. Jesus respects the fury of an Indian Ocean typhoon and the life-giving snow packs of the American West. The Stranger of Galilee has deep and warm compassion for children's hospitals everywhere, and the Mother Teresas of the world who are doing "it unto the least of these my brethren." *(Matthew 25:40)*

The Jesus I know understands the happiness, joy and passion of newlyweds everywhere, and the sorrow and pain that death brings to "old sweethearts" when earthly union ends after 60 years of love, friendship, and togetherness.

Jesus mourns for the wayward and sinners, and rejoices in those whose discipleship He knows to be sincere and genuine. He longs for the return of the prodigal sons and daughters, and is deeply moved by charity as He was at the temple in Jerusalem when the widow quietly shared her meager mite with the poor.

I believe Jesus loves the urchins in the great cities of the world as much as He does the ancient and modern prophets. He is not deeply impressed with the accumulation of wealth, and dismisses worldly fame and physical beauty as quite irrelevant. He will personally hold accountable for their actions those who hold great earthly powers in military, political, and economic realms.

I deeply believe that Jesus is aware of the events that occur in the world and in the lives of all mankind. I cannot explain, nor do I understand, the inequities of life, or why the playing field is so uneven for so many. I only wish I had those answers, but I am confident that someday He will provide them.

What I am sure of is that God the Father and Jesus Christ will be fair and demanding judges of each person's life and behavior. Obedience, accountability, and knowledge will be critical factors as they weigh our conduct in this mortal probation. What we receive as an eternal reward we will largely determine ourselves. God's judgement will be based upon the eternal principles of charity, kindness, love, mercy, divine justice, obedience and our service to others. I believe no man will be denied anything he has earned or deserves, and conversely, no one will be given a reward that is not rightfully his.

In the final judgment, as the omnipotent and omniscient judge, God will not be fooled by human deception, con artists, image, and human accomplishment that are irrelevant to divine law and experience. Each man and woman will be judged not by whether "they won or lost, but how they played the game," as Grantland Rice once wrote. Election to a "Hall of Fame" will count considerably less than the widow's mite.

For centuries men and women have painted portraits and sketched images of Jesus Christ. As noted earlier, these renditions cover a wide range of images. Some may closely represent His actual appearance while others are certainly far off the mark. How helpful and revealing it would be if we had a contemporary painting of Christ, or better still, a genuine photograph. Of course they do not exist, so mankind, with the exception of some prophets and worthy sons and daughters of God, will have to wait for His return to learn what He really looks like. When we see Him for the first time as a resurrected God, it is my belief that we will behold a ruggedly handsome individual who is a perfect specimen of manhood. He will be strong in appearance and yet kind and gentle in His countenance. His powerful and penetrating eyes will leave us with the realization that He not only sees us outwardly but looks deep into our souls. His voice will be strong, but reassuring.

As He embraces us, we will feel the power of His wounded hands and the strong arms that formed the earth, placed the moistened mud on the blind man's eyes, broke the bread that fed the 5,000, and lifted the sinking Peter from the Sea of Galilee. In His glorious person, we will sense His divine majesty, and realize how only He, as the Lamb without blemish, could be our Savior. His physical countenance and great power will convince each of us that His meekness and submission to those who forced Him to undergo the mockery of His trials and the incomprehensible experiences of Gethsemane and the cross at Calvary were driven by His complete obedience to His Father, and our Father, and His infinite love for each of us.

Let us now turn to Jesus Christ the defender of man's free agency, a divine gift that is God's second greatest gift to His children. Without it, we cannot reach the status Christ admonished us to achieve as recorded in the 48th verse of the 5th Chapter of Matthew. "Be ye therefore perfect, even as your Father which is in heaven is perfect." This divine and eternal principle and law of man's agency has existed from time immemorial.

God the Father has honored and followed it in all His dealings with His children. His strict adherence to it came not only from the fact that He too is bound by eternal and divine law, but by His ageless experience with human behavior.

God knew prior to the creation, and He knows now, that each of His children could achieve the greatest and highest eternal status only if he or she proved worthy of that gift. That worthiness could only be established and proven through the principle of obedience to divine law. Such obedience was and is meaningless without the freedom of each person to choose between right and wrong, good and evil, and God and Satan. Our Eternal Father knows that forced obedience would result in counterfeit perfection. Passage through the refiner's fire and the experience, and sometimes the agony, of making difficult choices are fundamental to the progress of mortal man. It is necessary for most of us to stare Lucifer square in the eye and choose between honesty and a lie, theft and respect for other's property, adultery and fidelity, and mammon and the things of God.

CHAPTER TWO

THE JESUS I KNOW IN HIS PREMORTAL LIFE

In the Councils of Heaven prior to the creation, this great eternal law of man's agency was one of the two major issues on the agenda. The other issue, whom would God choose and send to the earth as the Savior of mankind, was also closely tied to the law of free agency. Lucifer, who aspired to be the Savior, demanded an unacceptable price from God the Father if he were to perform that role. First, he insisted that the power and glory for saving mankind from their necessary mortal fall should be given to him and not the Father. Such arrogance and usurpation could never be accepted by God for obvious reasons. Foremost was the divine and accepted fact that God the Father exercises power, glory, and authority for the benefit and blessing of His children. He is a righteous holder and wielder of power. That is not the case with Lucifer. It was his desire and intent to use the power he would take from the Father for his own corrupt purposes. He had no real intention to bless his brothers and sisters who were the children of God. *(Rev 12:7-9; Abraham 3:24-28)*

When Christ spoke in that august assembly, His was a different message and agenda. He appreciated and understood fully the eternal laws under which His Father operated. Unlike His younger brother, He had no personal agenda, and especially no compulsive desire or plan to usurp power and glory from His Father. He knew that He and His brothers and sisters would share that power and glory with the

Father in the future if it were deservedly earned. He knew that such sharing of power could occur only in an environment of love, trust, respect, and obedience. Most critically, Christ knew that the difference between His offer to be the Messiah and Satan's offer would require God to sacrifice forever the eternal law of man's free agency. Man's freedom was as precious to Christ as it was to His Father.

Satan, of course, was a very sore loser. The Father's acceptance of Christ's offer to be the Savior of mankind led Satan to rebel against both his Father and his elder brother. The Son of the Morning chose rebellion rather than responsible compliance to his Father's will. Satan's action forced all of God's children to make a monumental and eternal decision. The consequences of what followed are not easily understood by us mere mortals.

As deeply as the Father loved all of His children, He would not and could not compromise the free agency of man which is divine, eternal, universal, and irrevocable law. He stood firm while Satan successfully convinced one-third of his brothers and sisters—all of whom were also Christ's brothers and sisters and children of our Heavenly Parents—to join him in open rebellion against God and Christ. The Father drew a clear line on the battleground of Heaven. He allowed Lucifer and his angels to exercise the very law they were trying to destroy.

The people who followed Lucifer chose wrongly and poorly; they decided to follow a man whose purposes, goals, and objectives then and now are evil, destructive, and excruciatingly painful. They chose to follow the greatest deceiver and con artist of all time and the most selfish man in recorded scripture and human history. They may not have fully understood the permanence and eternal consequences of their choice, but they certainly understood that it was between Satan and his forced and guaranteed salvation, and Christ's plan for each person to be the determinator of his or her eternal reward. To paraphrase Winston Churchill, "Never have so many been so wrong for so long."

We, of course, have few details about the War in Heaven. Whatever the battle plan and weapons, the outcome was never in doubt.

As we ponder that conflict we should never lose sight of the central issue. Rather than destroy or compromise the free agency of man, the Father was willing to lose, and cast from His presence forever, a third of His spiritual children. Divine law and eternal principles were more critical to Him than rebellious children who would destroy it. He paid an incredible price to preserve our agency. We should also never forget that in the war regarding our eternal freedom, Christ was our leader and the victor.

The reader should have surmised by now that the author not only deeply believes in Christ as the Holy Messiah, he also accepts with certainty the existence of Satan. Holy Scripture testifies of the existence of both. *(Isaiah 14:12; Revelation 12:7-9)*

Even if one cannot accept the divine mission of Christ, it seems that there is enough evil in the world to convince any reasonable soul that Satan really exists. Man's inhumanity to man, epitomized in the Twentieth Century by Hitler, Stalin, Mao, Pol Pot and the evil of today's terrorists should be convincing enough. If someone's mind is impervious to those evils, they need look no further than gang and drug warfare, the trash on television, and the evil of killing unborn children. Conversely, if one does not accept the existence of God and the mission of Jesus Christ, the dismissal of the existence of Satan is much easier. Once that false step is taken, the adherent then must somehow explain the indescribable evil which has occurred in the past and which goes on every day around the world.

Acceptance of Christ as the great law giver and the arbiter of what is moral, right or wrong, or good or evil gives us a compass whereby we may conduct our lives. He gives us a clear definition of evil, and of Satan and his allies. *(Alma 5:40-41)* The Jesus I know has drawn a line in the sands of time and defined for all mankind what conduct will make him or her a happy person and what conduct will make him or her miserable.

Few things, if any, epitomize evil more dramatically than the bitter and malignant emotion of hate. It has driven uncounted acts of human destruction throughout history, especially the malicious campaigns of Hitler against the Jews, Stalin against the Kulak peasants, and Pol Pot's capricious murder of nearly three million of his countrymen. This vicious human characteristic unfortunately leads to crimes against innocent individuals the world over. It becomes a poison to the human soul and ranks as one of Satan's most successful generators of violent human conduct.

I have personally seen and felt hatred in several of the old Balkan States where bitterness between different ethnic and religious peoples has festered for centuries. These factors were exacerbated greatly by the breakup of the former Yugoslavia in 1991-1992. The demagogurey of the Serbian President compounded the situation and resulted in a three-year war from 1992-1995 in Bosnia-Herzegovina. Horrible violence and "ethnic cleansing" occurred. In 1998-1999, ethnic Albanians were forced out of Kosovo by the Serbs into Albania and Macedonia.

The Church of Jesus Christ of Latter-day Saints was providing food for a refugee camp in Macedonia. As senior missionaries working with LDS Charities, my wife and I had the opportunity to travel there. Standing alongside the chain link fence which cordoned off the no-man's land between Kosovo and Macedonia through which the Kosovo Albanians were slowly and painfully walking to the check point at Camp Blace, we saw firsthand the victims of the Serbian hatred toward the Albanian Kosovars.

In the refugee camps, with the help of interpreters, we talked to numerous people who had lost family members, material possessions, and even their identity papers. Most of the adults expressed hatred toward the Serbs in a bitterness that was very difficult to understand. That bitterness was reciprocated by the Serbs toward the Kosovars. On farms and in refugee camps in Croatia, I have interviewed Bosnian Muslims and Christians whose hatred of Serbians was no less than what I found in Kosovo. Similar conditions exist in the Middle East where some Jews and Palestinians hate each other with an intensity and passion that makes Satan proud.

There is only one antidote to Satan's campaign of death and misery which hatred heaps upon mankind. Christ gave us the answer not once, but numerous times. We must love our neighbors as ourselves.

He requires us to forgive those who trespass against us and those who despitefully use us. The commandments are not always easy, and many societies and individuals disregard them, but they have never been repealed by the Master.

I can offer no better proof or witness of the superiority of Christ's way than to suggest to each reader to honestly weigh the times and events in his or her life when feelings of love and forgiveness reigned, compared to those occasions when hatred and bitterness captured the soul.

From the role of defender of man's agency, Christ next took on the assignment from His Father to create and organize the earth in preparation for our sojourn here. Unlike the Council and War in Heaven, which are known to us only through brief scriptural references from ancient and modern prophets, the creation is quite well documented in Genesis. It is also ours to tangibly see, observe, and experience practically every day of our lives. We forget sometimes that man's earthly existence is also governed by divine and natural law which requires us to live and exist with the forces of nature which God and Christ designed for this earth. Thus, we are subject to the earth's great productivity, natural forces, awesome beauty and sometimes its remarkably destructive power.

We benefit from water and the rays of the sun which sustain life by causing crops to grow. Conversely, in some regions of the earth, the sun scorches and burns where there is little or no water. We stand in awe of the beauty of a magnificent sunset over a barren desert, and tremble at the destructive power of a South Pacific typhoon or Hurricane Andrew in the Caribbean. We enjoy the beauty of a deep red rose, the splendor of an orchid, and the sweet delicious taste of an Elberta peach.

Most of us benefit from the incredible blessings of light, heat, air conditioning, and mobility, because Christ provided flowing rivers, coal deposits, and petroleum and gas reserves that drive the power generators and vehicles, ships, and aircraft of the world. Christ gave to us the spectacular beauty of Victoria and Niagara Falls, the highlands of Ethiopia, and the productive farms in Western Europe, the Ukraine, the American Midwest, and the great cattle ranches of Argentina.

He left for us the awesome spectacle of the Grand Canyon and the towering Himalayas. In the waters that cover much of the earth, He provided a wide variety of marine life to help feed the people of the world. Across the globe He gave us the Nile, the Rhine, the Amazon, the Mississippi, the Euphrates and numerous other tributaries to drain and water the land, and to provide in both early and modern times highways for the world.

He gave much of the earth seasons which bring us the beauty and renewed life of Spring with its countless flowers, trees, blossoms, and new hope that causes men and women to plant the fertile farm land of the world. He provided rain and sun, and nutrients in the soil which cause the ear of corn to mature, the rice and grain to ripen and the potatoes to grow. The miracle of the plant life which Christ provided gives a sweet aging grandmother in Ireland the great satisfaction of raising beautiful flowers, and the young farmer in Bangladesh success with his rice crop. The soil, the rain, the sun and the seasons continue their timeless cycles so that by the sweat of their brows, aided in our time by incredible science and technology, the noble farmers, ranchers and fishermen of the world continue to feed the people of the world.

In creating the earth, Christ gave to each of us an endless panorama of natural beauty. The radiant colors of fish in the oceans and the magnificent plumage of birds around the world are testaments of His love for sheer beauty. In the animal and wildlife kingdoms we behold the incredible aerodynamics of a humming bird and the sheer size and mass of an African elephant and a great Clydesdale draft horse. The magnificence and scope of the earth's wildlife and animal kingdom, the vastness of the oceans and seas of the globe, the productivity of the earth's farms, ranches and mines, and the vast reserves of timber, natural gas and oil, all whisper quietly, but assuredly, that it was the Master's hand, and His love and concern for each of us that caused Him to create it for us.

Only on a few occasions and environments did He make life easy for us. For most of us He requires that we husband wisely the resources of the earth. In our day, He has blessed mankind with incredible new technologies and much scientific progress that allows a cooperative partnership between the physical efforts required to plant and harvest the wheat, bake the bread and deliver it to those who use it as the staff of life.

We must never forget that Christ provided directly or indirectly every resource and product that mankind uses. The most powerful and modern computer, space shuttle or medical device was or is possible only by using the earth's vast natural resources. The bounties, beauty, order and blessings of the earth were and are His gift to all mankind. Unfortunately, our stewardship of His donated resources has not always been Christ like.

Chapter Three

Christ's Birth and Early Years

The birth of Jesus Christ is the most celebrated event in the Christian world, and is beautifully recorded and documented in Luke and the other gospels. The humble circumstances of Mary's conception and Christ's birth were designed by His Father and faithfully executed by Mary and Joseph. Christ's arrival upon the earth was meant to be the antithesis of a royal and kingly advent. The Savior of Mankind's birth in a lowly stable in Bethlehem was but the beginning of an earthly ministry that was bereft of worldly grandeur, pomposity, luxury and political power.

It would be most interesting and informative indeed if we had a record of Christ's life for the years between His return from Egypt with Joseph and Mary, and His 30th year when He began His brief three year ministry. For whatever reasons, the Gospel writers give us only a few details about those early years. We are told by Luke about His circumcision, which met the requirements of Jewish law, and His remarkable visit to the temple in Jerusalem during the family's Passover visit when Christ was 12 years of age. *(Luke 2)* Beyond those events, we have practically nothing recorded in Holy Scripture about His growing up years. We are entitled, I believe, to ask certain questions. Answers to those questions, of course, can only be speculation, but perhaps not far off the mark.

It is fair to assume that Jesus led the life of a normal child until He approached the age of 12. He certainly was tutored and educated in Jewish law and history as a boy. We can also safely assume that He was exceptionally bright and intelligent as a child and young boy because of His parents. Mary certainly stands among God's finest daughters. As His mother, she clearly possessed the divine attributes of love, kindness, compassion, nurturing, and understanding. She had to possess a fine mind, and was, I believe, a beautiful woman. Christ, of course, inherited the physical and mental attributes of His Father in Heaven who was the Father of both His spirit and His earthly body. Christ told us often in the scriptures that if you have seen me, you have seen the Father. *(John 14:9)*

I do not believe that fact prevented Him from going through the normal processes of infancy, childhood and His teens, although He must have been the only model teenager ever to have lived on the earth. I do not think it would be farfetched to assume that He engaged in the games and activities of a normal childhood. Maybe He raced His donkey against His young friends on the back roads of Nazareth. He certainly was swift afoot and very agile in the games of the neighborhood. I wonder if He did not like spinach or warm goat's milk, but loved honey on unleavened bread.

Did the boy Jesus one day walk into Joseph's carpenter shop, and tell His noble earthly guardian, "I can do it myself." At whatever age Joseph began to teach the Son of God the carpentry trade, we can assume his task was not a difficult one. He was teaching a boy who had earlier organized the great forests of Scandinavia. This boy, with His Father, was the lawgiver of physics and geometry, and the creator of the California Redwoods. Jesus was very familiar with teak, oak, pine, cherry, cedar and all varieties of wood.

We have no earthly record of what the young carpenter built. We can assume, I believe, that He was an eager and most capable apprentice under Joseph's watchful eye, and that He appreciated His stepfather's skill, patience, and loving instruction. His was a noble craft, and whatever Jesus constructed with His own hands—cabinets, chairs or houses—was certainly superior workmanship.

At this point let us take a brief detour and record some thoughts and impressions about Joseph and Mary. As is the case with so much of Christ's early life, we know very little about His mother and step-father. Mary's status as the woman chosen to be Christ's mother, her conception through the power of the Holy Ghost, and her pregnancy and delivery of the Christ child are well documented. *(Luke 1:34-35)* She was present and asked Christ to change the water into wine at the Canaan marriage feast. *(John 2:1-11)* Her presence at the crucifixion of her Savior Son is also noted in scripture. *(John 19:25-26)* That she performed well her divine mission as Christ's noble mother, not only in giving Him life but in nurturing Him to adulthood, is accepted in Heaven and throughout Christendom.

We know even less about the noble Joseph than we do Mary. That he was a man of great decency is recorded by Matthew:

> Now the birth of Jesus Christ was on this wise: When as his mother Mary was espoused to Joseph, before they came together, she was found with child of the Holy Ghost.
>
> Then Joseph her husband, being a just man, and not willing to make her a publick example, was minded to put her away privily.
>
> *Matthew 1:18-19*

We should never forget that Joseph was worthy to be Mary's earthly, and eternal husband. He was also worthy of important revelations from Heaven. While pondering what to do about Mary's pregnancy, for which he was not responsible, he was visited by a heavenly messenger in an emphatic dream. *(Matthew 1:18-25)* Joseph faithfully and explicitly obeyed the message of the angel to take Mary as his wife. Matthew's account notes that he "knew her not till she had brought forth her firstborn son." In Biblical language this simply means that he had no sexual relations with Mary until after Christ's birth.

Joseph, as the guardian and protector of his lovely wife and the infant Jesus, again proved his worthiness and receptivity to divine guidance when shortly after the birth of the Christ child, an angel that was perhaps the same messenger as before, warned him in a second dream to flee into Egypt to save the young boy's life from the wicked Herod. *(Matthew 2:13-15)* This he did without questioning the command. Joseph somehow, probably as a carpenter, earned a living in Egypt and provided for Mary and the Son of God. After Herod's death, a third messenger, again in a dream, directed the obedient Joseph to return to the land of Israel and to settle in Nazareth where according to prophecy Christ would live, and be called a Nazarene. *(Matthew 2:19-21).*

Before completing our consideration of Joseph's role in the life of Christ, we need to take another short but very important detour. Christ's Father is omnipotent and omniscient. Following His resurrection, Christ, too, had all those same attributes. As Christ grew in stature, and received grace upon grace, He certainly became aware of the deaths of His precious infant brothers and sisters slain by Herod while He was exiled in Egypt with Mary and Joseph. I deeply believe that He had great love for those infant victims and their parents. He shared the deep grief and sorrow of those helpless Jewish parents whose obedience to God's commandment to multiply and replenish the earth was punished by the brutal slaying of their cherished infants. They were helpless and broken hearted against Herod's heinous sin and crime. Their painful sacrifice Christ deeply felt, for He too would share the fate of their children at the hands of Roman power some 31 years later.

The slain victims of Bethlehem and the region thereabout were two years old or younger. *(Matthew 2:16)* Matthew's account notes that all children in that locality were slain, which infers that little girls as well as little boys were killed. Some were about to enter their terrible twos, some had just learned to walk, while others were still crawling on the rough floors of their humble homes. Some were still nursing at their mother's breasts. I believe Christ knew all of them by name and loved each one dearly. It is my firm conviction that following the necessary protocols of His return to His Father after His resurrection, or perhaps in the Spirit World between His crucifixion and triumphant victory over death, that He took Herod's innocent little victims in His arms and told each one that He loved him or her dearly, that He understood, and that all was well. I believe that same embrace, love, and divine assurance are given to every earthly child who passes prematurely through the valley of death. The Scriptures tell how deeply the Master loves children. His betrayal by Judas, His agonizing hours in the Garden of Gethsemane, His abusive trial and brutal crucifixion do not record the flow of tears from His penetrating eyes. But say the scriptures, He did weep when surrounded by little children who obviously touched Him very deeply. *(3 Nephi 17:21)*

Turning again to Joseph, we know very little about his personality, his role as Jesus' stepfather and where and how he fit into the Gospel and Church of Jesus Christ. Concerning his and Mary's deaths, we must wait for future revealed history. I believe our Father in Heaven chose Joseph to be Christ's earthly stepfather for several reasons. It is not an unwarranted position to assume that throughout His early years of mortal existence, Christ was protected and tutored by angels from Heaven. By the time He engaged the Jewish elders in the Temple, He was aware of His divine sonship and His Messianic mission. That knowledge and awareness came to Him in some manner from Heaven, perhaps through the spoken word of the Father's similar to the direct message given at the time of Christ's baptism. Perhaps it was through His Godhead colleague, the Holy Ghost, who possesses divine revelatory powers beyond man's understanding. God, however, seems to reserve earthly function for mere mortals; He did not build the ark for Noah nor the vessel for Lehi and his family. While He parted the Red Sea and sent manna from heaven for the children of Israel, tasks no mortal seemed capable of doing, He left Israel to fight its own wars, and David, not a heavenly warrior, slew Goliath. It is safe to conclude, therefore, that there were obviously certain things left for Joseph and Mary to do in the life of their divine Son. They were responsible for His daily needs as an infant and as a little boy. In their house He was taught to pray, the history of Israel, and the ancient scriptures, which He certainly recognized quickly since He was the source thereof. Mary dressed His scrapes and Joseph taught Him how to use the tools of the carpentry craft. Certainly they taught

Him, as well as their other children, the principles of honesty, kindness, love and forgiveness. In their home, Jesus learned to live in harmony with His brothers and sisters.

After their temple experience with Jesus at age twelve, Mary and Joseph would spend the next 18 years loving Him and sharing His life, while perhaps not fully comprehending the events which He would experience at the end of His mortal ministry. From age twelve onward, He knew who He was and generally what His earthly mission would require. In all probability, He could not fully share them with His devoted and sweet mother and the noble Joseph.

We can assume that they saw great change in their Son as He grew from grace to grace, and that one day as He neared His 30th birthday, there was a tender and loving farewell. Perhaps by now, they at least knew that their Son was the Holy Messiah. If He ever returned home again after He started His ministry, it is not recorded. In a sense, He was no longer theirs. He belonged to His Father in Heaven and all His brothers and sisters who had and would spend time on the earth He had created for them. When He left Nazareth, the world and all its people would be changed forever. Whether they fully understood His Holy Messiahship, Joseph and Mary had performed well the responsibilities given to them by their Father in Heaven. She had given Him life; Joseph had saved His life, and He was, with their help, ready to become the Savior of Mankind. Their stewardships were noble and faithfully performed.

Chapter Four

Christ and His Relationships with People

The sum of human existence is centered on relationships between individuals. Not even the occasional hermit or the unfortunate loner can completely escape this requirement of life. Theories, models, counselor guidance, laws, seminars, courses, clergy, courts, and legislative bodies have all with varying degrees of success tried to teach and define the basis of human relationships.

Human beings conduct interpersonal relationships that range from brutal war and angry savagery to precious love, pure kindness, and lasting friendship and respect for others.

Most people want to believe that we are making progress in dealing with each other. Hopefully there will be no more of Hitler's Jewish Solution, or Stalin's slaughter of the Kulaks, or American slavery, or Pol Pot's killing fields, or the ethnic hatred and killing in Bosnia and Kosovo by Serbs and Muslims alike. In the Western world, most of us have fortunately escaped such brutal atrocities, and hopefully such horrible events can eventually be stopped in our modern world.

Much of the focus of failed human relationships appears now to be centered on drug and criminal behavior, terrorism, rebellion against despotic governments, broken families, gang conflicts, and spouse and child abuse. As civilized and not so civilized societies struggle with the problems of failed human relations, we should be grateful indeed for the vast majority of people who conduct themselves in a civilized and

Christlike fashion. We should have no illusions, however, that evil and degrading human behavior will be completely removed from the world before Christ returns in majestic power, because Lucifer is very powerful and has too many agents in his employ. Such stark reality does not remove from each of us the responsibility to conduct our lives in a peaceful manner and to give each person we deal with the respect and courtesy they deserve. Indeed, the admonition of Christ to "love thy neighbor as thyself" *(Leviticus 19:18)*, and "whatsoever ye would that men should do to you, do ye even so to them" *(Matthew 7:12)* are most basic to human relations. Simple observance of these two principles would change human relations throughout the world almost instantly, and impose on Satan an almost irreversible set back. But don't hold your breath!

As indicated earlier, Christ's primary mission was to save mankind from the fall of Adam and the spiritual and physical separation from God which that fall caused. Another mission was to bring the saving and exalting principles and ordinances, and the authority to administer them to the world. A third mission of the Savior was to teach by word and deed the Gospel principles that would offer to each of us true discipleship.

I would like to turn now to the deeds of Christ which serve as an example to each of us as we deal with our brothers and sisters and fellow human beings. His deeds and actions were always as powerful and exemplary as His words.

As an introduction, let us review briefly our debt to Adam and Eve. The events that occurred in the Garden of Eden are not always understood by Christians. To many followers of Jesus Christ, Adam and Eve committed a grievous sin when they partook of the forbidden fruit. That act, they believe, brought original sin to mankind and left us in a state of degradation. To them Adam and Eve were less than noble progenitors. That view and interpretation of our first parents is far off the mark.

In the pre-existence, Adam was Michael the Archangel, and in that role assisted Christ in the creation and organization of the earth. *(Rev 12:7; D&C 27:11)* We must therefore assume that Adam's performance in the spirit world was stellar indeed. He had proven himself as a trusted, capable, and obedient son of God. Our Father in Heaven's decision to place him at the head of the human race and make him the first man on earth was certainly deserved. Eve's status as the first woman, and Adam's wife, also reflected great respect and trust of her as a noble and obedient daughter of our Heavenly Parents.

Once Adam and Eve were formed physically from the elements of the earth and placed in the Garden of Eden, God the Father and Jesus Christ implemented their divine and far reaching plan that would govern the existence of mankind on the earth from beginning to end. That plan was based on specific eternal and divine principles.

- As a resurrected glorified being, our Heavenly Father wanted to share that status and all that He had with His children who had remained valiant and faithful during the War in Heaven. For God to share His gifts with His obedient spirit children, each had to receive a physical body and undergo an earthly probation.
- The eternal principle of man's agency would never be compromised or violated. As noted earlier, it was the primary cause of the War in Heaven where it was preserved at great cost. In the Garden of Eden and in the earth life of God's children, it would also be carefully guarded against Satan's ceaseless and evil efforts. *(2 Nephi 2:27; D&C 29:36)*
- Satan was a terribly sore loser and after the War in Heaven was banished to the earth as a spirit without a body. He and his disciples were permitted to tempt Adam and Eve, and their posterity, but he was not permitted to violate or destroy their agency. Unfortunately, countless descendants of Adam and Eve have lost their agency through their own actions by choosing to disobey God's laws, thus becoming slaves to an evil master.
- When Adam and Eve were initially placed in the Garden of Eden, their bodies were immortal and not subject to death. As long as they did not partake of the forbidden fruit as God had commanded, they would not die.

- The second of God's commandments to Adam and Eve was to multiply and replenish the earth. If they obeyed the first commandment concerning the forbidden fruit, then they could not obey this directive and bear children. God fully understood their dilemma, because He was the author of it. It was His will and desire that Adam and Eve exercise their free agency and choose to obey one or the other of the commandments. He also knew that as intelligent and perceptive children, Adam and Eve would quickly understand that the child bearing commandment was the critical one, and that the forbidden fruit prohibition would simply allow them to exercise their divine right of free agency and set in motion the process of man's mortal probation.
- Satan, bless his vicious and evil soul, conducted himself just as God the Father knew he would. He told some magnificent lies to Adam and Eve and also taught a simple truth. The scriptures tell us that this master deceiver could not initially convince Adam to eat the forbidden fruit, but he did succeed with Eve, who responded to Satan's truthful logic that she would know good from evil and be able to keep the greater commandment to bear children. *(Genesis 3:1-5)* Had Adam and Eve refused to partake of the fruit, they would still be cavorting naked in the Garden of Eden, not knowing good from evil, childless and thwarting the desires of God. The Prophet Lehi has described their situation as succinctly as anyone. "Adam fell that man might be; and men are, that they might have joy." *(2 Nephi 2:25)*

There is a great lesson of trust to be learned from God's relations with Adam and Eve in the Garden. The Father trusted them to make the right decision when confronted with conflicting commandments or choices. That trust He also grants to each of us if we choose to exercise it. We do not, of course, confront a choice between the forbidden fruit and child bearing as our first parents did. Our choices in most cases are between good and evil, right and wrong, a lot of gray areas, but ultimately between Christ and Satan. We sometimes choose evil over good, dishonesty over honesty, adultery over fidelity, tobacco over Brussels sprouts, and alcohol over orange juice. God loves us nevertheless, and keeps working and hoping that as we progress through life, our right decisions will eventually outnumber our wrong decisions. Our Father in Heaven and our Savior do not easily give up on us.

Few things in the life of Christ are more revealing about His personality than His interactions and interrelationships with specific people. His debate and verbal exchanges with the Pharisees and the Sadducees give us insight into how deeply He despised hypocrisy and phoniness. His answer to the rich young ruler to sell all that he had and give the proceeds to the poor reflected a degree of frustrating impatience. His combination of silence, terse, but truthful replies before the Jewish Sanhedrin and before Herod and Pilate, who would decide His fate, were great displays of divine dignity. Christ's counsel to His disciples to render unto Caesar that which was Caesar's and to God that which was God's, was a timeless example of historical perspective and wisdom. *(Mark 12:15-17)*

That the Stranger of Galilee was capable of being impatient with apostles and disciples whose faith was not yet strong was clearly demonstrated when He fed the multitudes of 5,000 and 4,000, and when they were unable to heal the sick and raise the dead. *(Matt 15:32-38; 17:18-21)*

We touch here briefly on Christ's dealings with several people. Most of them will be further considered later in this narrative, not from Christ's perspective, but from theirs. Jesus demonstrated great respect and love for the widow who quietly and without any outward demonstration cast a lowly mite in the temple treasury. He made her a righteous legend in the annals of true charity. *(Mark 12:42-44)* To the one leper who returned to express thanks for being healed, Jesus was of course appreciative of his gesture, but did not avoid expressing His disappointment that the other nine were quite ungrateful. To all that He healed, the Master showed great compassion, love and understanding. More than any other person who had walked the earth, He understood the curse of leprosy, the stillness of the deaf and the darkness of those who could not see the sunset or behold the splendor of a lily. To the hopeless sinner and the wayward soul, He expressed hope, compassion and trust as He taught the eternal truths of the Parables of the Lost Sheep and the Prodigal Son. *(Luke 15:4-7)*

Thirsting at Jacob's well in Samaria, He taught the woman from the village that she, too, was a daughter of God and worthy of inclusion in the Church of Christ. To her, and to Peter whom He gave the great gentile vision, He spoke of acceptance and love of all mankind regardless of race, origin or history. *(John 4:5-43)*

As He walked a dusty road enroute to Jairus' home in Capernaum, He showed again that He had great compassion for the downtrodden. Perceiving that virtue had gone out of Him, He turned, despite protestations and feeble efforts of crowd control by His disciples, and changed forever the life of the humble woman afflicted with a blood disease, who had so much faith that by merely touching the hem of Christ's garment was made whole. Jesus not only healed her, He loved her and showed how deeply He respected her faith. *(Mark 5:25-34)*

To Mary and Martha He showed that He understood certain things in life were more important than others.

> Now it came to pass, as they went, that he entered into a certain village: and a certain woman named Martha received him into her house.
>
> And she had a sister called Mary, which also sat at Jesus' feet, and heard his word.
>
> But Martha was cumbered about much serving, and came to him, and said, Lord, dost thou not care that my sister hath left me to serve alone? bid her therefore that she help me.
>
> And Jesus answered and said unto her, Martha, Martha, thou art careful and troubled about many things:
>
> But one thing is needful: and Mary hath chosen that good part, which shall not be taken away from her.
>
> *Luke 10:38-42*

Christ demonstrated that He was a thoughtful and appreciative recipient of kindnesses provided. Momentarily Martha was more concerned about her role as hostess than the service she chose to give. Christ ever so gently complimented her as He reinforced Mary's choice. We should not forget, however, that without Martha there would have been no supper.

When Lazarus died his two faithful sisters expressed to the Savior identical statements: "Lord, if thou hadst been here, my brother had not died." *(John 11: 21, 32)* They further acknowledged the reality of the resurrection made possible by their dear friend Jesus Christ the Son of God. The Savior knew He was going to restore Lazarus back to a mortal life and that Mary and Martha would soon enjoy his company. However, as they mourned Lazarus' death He wept with them. This family deeply felt the Savior's compassion and witnessed His divinity. *(John 11:1-46)*

Except for His long relationship with Peter, I believe there is no recorded interpersonal relationship as touching and meaningful as Christ had for a brief moment with the woman who had been taken in adultery. To this guilty and frightened woman, He showed compassion, love and firmness. He also used the occasion to once again demonstrate His deep hatred of hypocrisy. I should like to review this great episode at this point in the narrative since Christ, not the woman, was the principal figure.

Returning to the temple in Jerusalem from the Mount of Olives early one morning, Jesus was teaching the assembled crowd when certain Pharisees and scribes brought to Him a woman who had been taken in the very act of adultery. Two things are remarkable about their initial appearance. For whatever reason, the man involved in the adulterous act was left out of the episode by the woman's accusers. He apparently would be answerable only to God, although Christ certainly knew his identity, as He does the identity of all sinners. On this occasion, the scribes and Pharisees once again operated under a double standard. Secondly, in their own hypocritical minds, they were certain that they had chosen the right circumstance for maximum embarrassment, not so much for the woman, but for Jesus. How could this Galilean heretic, they reasoned, fail to uphold their narrow interpretation of the Mosaic Law before a crowd of people assembled in the temple?

The dialogue between these self-righteous hypocrites and Jesus before the people recorded in the Gospel of John is most revealing of Christ's powers of perception and His insight into human behavior. Using the title Master, which they used most insincerely, their spokesman told Jesus that:

> This woman was taken in adultery, in the very act.
>
> Now Moses in the law commanded us, that such should be stoned: but what sayest thou?
>
> This they said, tempting him, that they might have to accuse him. But Jesus stooped down, and with his finger wrote on the ground, as though he heard them not.
>
> So when they continued asking him, he lifted up himself, and said unto them, He that is without sin among you, let him first cast a stone at her.
>
> And again he stooped down and wrote on the ground
>
> And they which heard it, being convicted by their own conscience, went out one by one, beginning at the eldest, even unto the last: and Jesus was left alone, and the woman standing in the midst.
>
> When Jesus had lifted up himself, and saw none but the woman, he said unto her, Woman where are thine accusers? hath no man condemned thee?
>
> She said, No man Lord, And Jesus said unto her, Neither do I condemn thee: go and sin no more.
>
> *John 8:4-11*

Only occasionally did a Gospel writer record an event so revealing of Christ's nature and His relationship with His brothers and sisters as John did here.

Let us turn first to the woman's accusers. Those men, self-proclaimed defenders and judges of Israel's moral code, were determined to discredit the Master. How they found the woman in her adulterous act is not recorded, but whether they had been looking for such a violation of the seventh commandment or discovered the event by accident, it was quickly recognized by these hypocrites as a rare opportunity of entrapment against Jesus, whom they knew was at the temple teaching the multitude. The scribes and Pharisees arrived, woman in hand, having previously conspired how to confront Jesus.

Their spokesman's words paid hollow deference to Moses and the law covering adultery. Those words were not only meant to entrap Jesus, they were also spoken to the assembled people who understood well the laws of Israel regarding this sin. Death by stoning was not foreign to that crowd. Public opinion, as the Pharisees and scribes knew, was a powerful force in Jerusalem. The spokesman's reference to Jesus as "Master" was pure hypocrisy, and by using it, the speaker intended to create in the minds of those present the impression that Jesus was the interpreter and arbiter of Jewish law. If the "Master" agreed and told them to stone the woman, He would be viewed as nothing more than a concurring rabbi. Conversely, if Jesus revoked the penalty regarding adultery, the multitude would, they reasoned, be shocked by His reversal of Moses. These scribes and Pharisees were so certain that they had finally trapped Jesus that some had carried a stone to the temple confrontation. For Christ's reply and response, they were completely unprepared. It is worthy of restatement, "He that is without sin among you, let him first cast a stone at her." *(John 8:7)*

Not a single scribe or Pharisee had the audacity to say to all assembled that "I am sinless." Shame, embarrassment, humiliation do not adequately describe those men as they left, according to John "beginning with the eldest unto the last." Stones that moments earlier were intended for the adulterous woman's body were quickly dropped, placed in a robe pocket or concealed behind clenched fists.

Whatever Christ had written on the ground was closely related to His convicting utterance. Some Biblical scholars have pontificated that He publicly documented specific sins of the accusers. Seldom during

His ministry had the intellectual equation with His enemies and detractors been so imbalanced. But the scribes, Pharisees and Sadducees never learned that Christ's single intellect was infinitely superior to their collective minds. That fact, however, did not deter them. They would press on despite the intellectual odds until they would convince Pilate to order the crucifixion of Jesus.

The accusing scribes and Pharisees are fortunately not the most critical story in John's account. Christ's remarks and personal interaction with the woman after the hypocrites had departed are the great lessons for all disciples of the Master.

Not only had the woman's accusers departed, but the multitude being taught by Jesus had apparently left also. Rising to His feet, Christ asked:

> Woman, where are those thine accusers? hath no man condemned thee?
>
> She said, No man, Lord, And Jesus said unto her, Neither do I condemn thee: go, and sin no more.
>
> *John 8:10-11*

Much more occurred here than a short exchange of words between Jesus and the nameless woman. The Master's reverse entrapment of her accusers had saved her from a brutal and painful death. She clearly was deeply relieved as the scribes and Pharisees departed, for she knew then that her life had been spared. That she was guilty of committing adultery was never in dispute, for even Jesus in closing the incident, admonished her to go and sin no more.

The most touching moment of the encounter with the Son of God was her receipt of Christ's loving and tender decision not to condemn her. I sincerely believe that as He spoke to her, Jesus looked deep into her soul and conveyed to her, and all who would read the account, the sublime peace of divine love and forgiveness.

She left the temple almost certainly alone, with her life spared, great inner peace and a solemn warning from the Master, "Go and sin no more." Her eternal standing in God's Kingdom was now in her own hands.

Chapter Five

Jesus and Those We Love

Our Families

God and Christ have revealed only tidbits of information to the world concerning the order and organization of the Heavens. We know from scripture that there are multiple kingdoms and countless mansions. *(John 14:2; D&C 59:2; 1 Cor 15:40-41)* We can certainly safely assume that the God who gave such precise and perfect order to the universe and our small planet has established order in the Heavens where we will live for eternity. That said, He has not told us if there will be branches, wards or stakes, not even a hint that BYU will exist. What He has told the world is that families are forever. That doctrine and divine practice started in the Garden of Eden when God married Adam and Eve and told them to have a family. He reiterated it in the Ten Commandments when He required each person to honor his or her father and mother. It was reinforced by Malachi when he foretold the sealing of one generation to another. Eternal families became even more established when Joseph Smith and the successor prophets began the process of building temples and doing genealogical research. What then does Jesus' gift of the family mean to us?

It starts with romance and the grand experience of falling in love. That special sweetheart becomes our lover and usually our best friend. Jesus ordained that we should undergo the divine experience of being co-creators with God by giving life and physical bodies to the spirit children of our Heavenly Parents.

The plan of eternal families requires us to face the challenges of marriage and parenthood. That means both joy and happiness and sometimes struggle and heartbreak. It entails the joy and pain of a wife giving birth to a healthy child and sometimes the heartbreak of a miscarriage and the loss of a precious child. It is messy diapers, the first step, cutting teeth and ear infections. It is the giggle of a wild two-year old and the tears brought on by a scraped knee.

Family life is the terrible twos, the innocence of being eight years old, and the challenge of being (and raising) teenagers. It is trust, friendship and the incredible experience of growing up and choosing between Satan's world and Christ's world.

Regardless of the stages we go through as families, it hopefully and usually comes to a time when a teenage son puts his arms around his Dad and they express to each other a strong love and friendship. It sometimes comes to a daughter telling friends at school that if she accepted the offer of alcohol or a cigarette that her Dad would kill her, knowing full well that he loved her and would not do such a thing, but for her it was a graceful and effective defense against evil. Her friends did not know the real truth, but they soon learned not to tempt her for fear of what her father would do.

Families are soccer and football games, swimming meets and yard work, family vacations whose memories linger for years, and old station wagons or vans which become part of family traditions. Families are school graduations, missionary farewells and temple marriages, gatherings where grown children confess their youthful pranks and parents confess the doubts and frustrations that turned into pride and respect for children who succeeded despite parental concerns. Families are precious grandchildren who allow grandparents to chuckle that their own children are now both required and blessed to be raising teenagers.

Sooner or later the twilight years come to every couple. Illness and disease sometimes cut short the golden years. For most of us these years bring deeper love, the peace and contentment of sharing a warm fire or a favorite movie viewed for the 25th time.

In God's family plan, death sometimes comes at an unexpected hour, or before one is ready. Sometimes He leaves us to linger far beyond our physical capacity to enjoy mortality. Regardless of when death comes, God and Christ have given us the assurance that human existence does not end. Our person is not consigned to nothingness. We have been assured that family members and loved ones live beyond death, and that departed family members and earthly survivors will see and know each other in the hereafter and the eternities to come. This assurance, as we bid a painful farewell at the funeral home and say a final tearful good-bye at the graveside, is one of God's most worthwhile blessings to His mortal children.

Christ and Little Children

Of all the personal relationships recorded in scripture between Christ and the people with whom He interacted, none is as touching and precious as those with little children. In their presence, He found a level of joy and peace that caused Him to weep. In Jerusalem, and in the land of Bountiful during His brief visit to America following His resurrection, He assembled the little children and blessed them in a most incredible way. *(3 Nephi 17:21-22; Luke 18:15-17)*

Jesus touched and undoubtedly embraced the children, and in Bountiful, He called down angels and a ring of fire wherein the angels ministered to them. What is it about a child that so touched the Master, who had a perfect knowledge of human nature and knows the hearts and souls of all men and women? No one, of course, cons Jesus Christ, who knows that children are honest, genuine and innocent. To each of us He explained that we must have the faith and innocence of a little child before we can enter the Kingdom of Heaven.

Let us take a moment and review some of the characteristics of children which make them so precious and which moved Christ to the point of tears.

A newborn child has only recently left the presence of his Father and Mother in Heaven, bringing the purity and innocence of that holy sphere to this world. God has decreed that the miracle of pro-creation be reserved for the institution of marriage. In today's world that decree is violated with relentless frequency and impunity, a fact which does not repeal the decree. Sexual union makes a husband and wife co-creators with God.

What endeared children to Jesus, to crusty old grandpas, and still tender-hearted grandmas? What is it about them that melts the hearts of mothers and fathers? Let me try to capture the spirit and essence of a child.

First, we should recognize that every child possesses a beautiful nature. As Sister Maria said in *The Sound of Music*, "Let's start at the very beginning." Ranked among the great beauties of the world is a new born.

Second, we know from experience that each child possesses a divine beauty. Lost in the tabulations of eternity is the number of times a just delivered mother has uttered the words, "She is so beautiful." This beauty which is present at birth just keeps growing, and pretty soon it takes on a personality that turns a helpless little boy into a human being of extraordinary dimensions. Comparable to a child's beauty is his or her innocence. By the time she is two, we sometimes wonder if the innocence of birth and infancy has been lost somewhere among the messed diapers, the countless feedings, and the gazillion episodes of joy radiating from this little lady. What is cuter in this world than a cherubic face, a plump little tummy, a fat little bum, and the sparkling eyes of a six-month old baby?

Third, the emergence of a little baby's personality is a joy to behold. Sooner or later this angel discovers the voice inside and the smile on the outside. She learns to coo and jabber before learning to talk, but someday that voice will comfort her own children, teach a primary class, and perhaps become an accomplished vocalist. Then there is the smile, a gift directly from God. It starts as a small movement of the mouth, and over the months and years evolves into a tool that disarms, enchants and charms adults. It says to all who see it, "I am happy and life is good in this little mortal tabernacle." It becomes a ray of sunshine, a moonbeam, and the easiest, most effective human expression.

Fourth, independence and curiosity invariably come to the fore. Somewhere along the way the hair grows. It may be black and strait, blond and curly, or red and vibrant. Mothers curl and comb it, wash it hundreds of times before the kid finally says, "I can get shampoo in my eyes by myself." Pretty soon the fingers and hands are discovered and then the toes. Not content to use them for their real purpose, the fingers sooner or later find their way into the mouth of the child and into Grandpa's nostril. What is going on in a baby's mind as he stares at his index finger for hours?

And finally, a new infant is an incredible source of joy. We cannot possibly dismiss the indescribable joy that comes to mom and baby from cuddling. It probably gives some kind of reassurance to the child and a feeling of joy, peace, and love to the mom. Whatever the respective emotions, it is one of life's great treasures. In describing the joy of a child, there are no doubt a lot of things that could be said, but does anything exceed the excitement and joy of a bath? At least when the kid wants to have a bath. In that warm water, a little boy sometimes turns into a sea monster. Splashing and getting water all over dad and the floor is a right guaranteed by family tradition. Though the joy and exuberance sometimes disappear when the hair washing ritual begins, it quickly returns when the suds are gone and the eyes are dried. Alas the joy begins to fade as the warm soapy water goes down the drain, but at least the little guy is clean for a while.

Not too far along in this process of infancy comes the experience of being comforted and relieved. It comes when the hunger pangs are placated, and the howling that far exceeds the size of the kid diminishes. It is a welcome separation from the wet diaper, or the tender wiping away of a tear or a runny nose. Being held firmly and warmly by a loving mom is compensation for all the discomforts of being a little kid.

Ah! The age of discovery for a child, it will last a lifetime and starts with fingers, toes, and other parts of that cute little body. Pretty soon it will include light, the toys hanging in the crib and grandma's earrings. Then it will include mom's kitchen drawers and the joy of messing in one's food. Bottles with warm milk will soon be tucked under an arm enroute to a nap, where the last few drops will be dribbled over the side of the crib onto the carpet in the first real experience with gravity. Not too far down the road this little genius will graduate from pure discovery to the "3-m's" of childhood — "monumental mess making."

It will include toys, clothes, cooking utensils and food spread all over the high chair and the floor, not to mention that precious little kisser. This habit, acquired in early infancy, is sometimes not broken or conquered before the early twenties and sometimes plagues the owner throughout mortality.

When exactly the "imp" characteristic sets in, one cannot say with surety, but set in it does. It seems to be tied to his or her little brain which sends the message that "I'm not quite the angel you think I am." It is sometimes accompanied by a wry smile, a blank stare or "catch me if you can" expression. It is personified by a five-year old turning off Grandpa's TV set in the final minutes of a close NBA game and then flexing his muscles challenging every adult in the room.

We adults could not bear an offspring's infancy without the existence of trust. We are not talking about us trusting them;, it is about them trusting us. We need it, and they take it for granted. They trust us with their lives, their fragile bodies and the development of their mind and personality. Mom and dad and other adults are their security and their safe havens in a crisis. When a dad holds his little guy up in the air on one hand, that boy has no fear of breaking his arm or bashing his head on the floor. Trust in his dad shows in his face more than if it were written in magic marker across his forehead. This child-centered trust is divinely instilled in a child and for the adults who must provide it, it is also a divine responsibility.

Perhaps determination and enthusiasm should be considered jointly. There are numerous things that could be said about these infant characteristics, but few things a child does exemplifies them better than the process of learning to walk. Transitioning a child from a helpless blob to mobile crawler to upright walker is a process that is really worth watching. It is a process of hundreds of failures and slow but measured success. Those first inches in a sweet girl's crawl are reflected in her look of smug satisfaction. Then comes the struggle to stand alongside an anchor of some kind. The Creator built a perfect design by putting the padded end at a point where it did not have far to fall to the surface and where the extra padding, both manmade and natural, serves as an effective shock absorber. Probably no one has kept track of bum first crash landings, but they are a necessary exercise in making a baby mobile.

It is one of the great joys in life to watch a little boy take his first steps. The combination of enthusiasm that got him there and that incredible look of accomplishment is choice indeed. Sometimes after the second or third step when upright mobility seems assured, the expression changes to a short, but real declaration of childish independence. "Hey, Mom, a few strands of your apron strings have been cut."

We'll close this section with a not so effective description of the "stare." Probably not all kids do it, but once in a while, one comes along that looks right through you. I've never been sure if they were telling us that "I am a real person," "take note of me," or "you are really a big dummy." Perhaps the little gal I know was saying, "I am special," or "do not mess with me," or "watch it, big fellow." Whatever they feel or sense, the stare is one adult characteristic that has been adopted by some unique little people.

The Jesus I know loves little children. No wonder He blessed them, and called down fire and angels to minister to them. It is not hard to understand why they caused the Son of God to weep.

CHAPTER SIX

CHRIST AND THE APOSTLE PETER

Peter is one man in Holy Scripture with whom most of us can relate. Like many scriptural figures, his personality, human weaknesses, and his remarkable accomplishments were recorded in part for our benefit. Consequently, we can trace at least part of his life history from his days as an unlettered, and perhaps unlearned, fisherman of Galilee, to his position as Chief Apostle and earthly leader of the Church after Christ's ascension into Heaven.

In reviewing Peter's relationship with the Master, it is clear that Jesus knew that Peter was a "diamond in the rough." President Spender W. Kimball calls him such in his discourse "Peter, My Brother" Speech of the Year presented at Brigham Young University in 1971. It is not, therefore, a disservice to Peter to say that he was a "personal project" of Christ that succeeded remarkably well.

Peter needed and underwent considerable molding and development as is obvious from even a cursory reading of the four Gospels and the Book of Acts. Peter was oftimes impetuous, stubborn, and slow to learn a lesson or understand a critical revelation. We must not forget in this narrative that the doctrines and principles that Christ was teaching to Peter, and the other apostles, were so new and different that time, repetition, and patience were critical elements in the process.

Frequently in his relationship with Jesus, Peter professed boldness and bravado that were quickly followed by fear and behavior that he came to deeply regret. Because of his personality, he, unlike most of the other apostles and disciples, was often the object of Christ's admonition, chiding, and occasional chastising. Peter the fisherman represents a marvelous combination of human frailty, personal strength, and measured progress. Most of us can relate to these characteristics without too much difficulty. While few, if any of us, will be an apostle, all of us can be a disciple. Each of us is capable of duplicating in many ways Peter's life: we have weaknesses and we have strengths, and by following and working with Christ through prayer, the scriptures, and persistent effort, we too are capable of great progress, and we should never forget that Christ loves each of us as much as He does Peter. Let us return now to the New Testament and examine in some detail the unique relationship between the fisherman of Galilee and the Carpenter from Nazareth.

As His ministry unfolded, Christ knew that He would need assistance in organizing His Church, preaching the Gospel to the known world, and administering the ordinances thereof. This assistance would be even more necessary after He returned to His Father in Heaven at the end of His earthly ministry. Sometime in the early months of His public ministry, Jesus went to the shore of the Sea of Galilee and met there two brothers, Simon called Peter and Andrew, who were casting their nets into the water. Matthew and Mark's accounts are much more abbreviated than Luke's and John's, both of whom note that Andrew and Peter had sought the Master after having heard John the Baptist preach. The consequence of their meeting was that Jesus asked Simon and Andrew to follow Him, and He would make them fishers of men. Matthew tells us that these two sons of Jona "straightway left their nets and followed him." At about that time He also called James and John to be fishers of men. *(Matthew 4:18-22)* Thus our first introduction to Peter and Andrew was this great act of faith and total obedience on their part. Peter's discipleship was never in doubt from that moment in history.

Jesus eventually called and ordained twelve men from among His disciples to serve as the original Twelve Apostles. *(Luke 6:12-16)* From the moment of their call, the Savior patiently taught, molded and prepared Peter and his eleven colleagues for their ministry, a process that would require much time and effort by the Master.

After Jesus had fed the 5,000 by miraculously expanding the five loaves and two fishes into enough food for the multitude, Christ sent His disciples, including Peter, to the opposite shore of the sea in a boat that probably belonged to one of the group. Jesus, after sending the 5,000 on their way, had retired to a nearby mount to pray to His Father. After this period of prayer was completed, the Master decided to join His disciples on the opposite shore. The voyage across the sea, though not far, was not made quickly nor without an element of fear and danger. Matthew tells us that "the ship was now in the midst of the sea, tossed with waves, for the wind was contrary." *(Matthew 14:24)*

During the fourth watch, Jesus approached the boat walking on the water. As He neared the craft, His presence brought fear to the group, but Jesus quickly identified himself. "Be of good cheer; it is I; be not afraid." *(Matthew 14:27)* Christ's presence and His miraculous mastery of the laws of nature emboldened the senior apostle. For a brief moment, Peter exhibited great faith, asking the Master "Lord, if it be thou, bid me come unto thee on the water." *(Matthew 14:28)* No such request was forthcoming from anyone else in the boat. Only Peter, it seems, was capable of such faith in Jesus, and such spontaneous behavior. The Master's answer was brief, "Come," He said, knowing the heart and soul of this former fisherman. Peter's great faith lasted but a few steps. The wind and the waves quickly overtook his temporary defiance of gravity and natural law as we understand it, and he began to sink. He cried "Lord, save me," which Jesus graciously and quickly did by taking Peter's hand and sustaining him until they were safely in the boat. To all occupants of the vessel, Christ walking on the water was an incredible thing to behold. His saving of Peter was equally miraculous, as was Jesus commanding power over the elements. I believe the event was one of many that would endear Peter to the Master who found it necessary to ask "O thou of little faith, wherefore didst thou doubt?" *(Matthew 14:31)*

Peter's remarkable experience which combined great faith, the eagerness of a young boy, and the divine powers of the Savior did not turn Peter into a shy, passive observer during the remaining months of the Master's ministry. To his credit, he placed his faith in Christ and for a brief moment he did walk on water. When the forces of nature caused his faith to falter and be replaced by fear and doubt, he had the good sense to turn to the only one present who could save him.

Many of us have had experiences similar to Peter. We have tried to exercise great faith, only to be overcome by doubt and fear as we faced the realities of adversity, opposition, and the stress of life. As Peter climbed into the ship with his robe soaking wet and his pride battered, he undoubtedly had a few moments to ponder his situation. Probably some of his friends put their arms around him, and perhaps one or two even snickered at his experience. What others thought, however, did not matter. Unlike his colleagues, he had tried and briefly succeeded. He was alive, and though he may have been embarrassed, he proved his boldness, his faith, and his leadership. From that hour, he was certainly much closer to the Son of God who had called him to be a "fisher of men" and saved him from being a long distance swimmer or a casualty of the sea and elements.

Peter's next reported "experience" with Jesus occurred sometime after the Master had fed the 4,000 by again greatly expanding the seven loaves and a few small fishes. While teaching and healing in Caesarea Philippi, Jesus asked His disciples,

> Whom do men say that I the Son of Man am?
>
> And they said, some say that thou art John the Baptist: some, Elias; and others, Jeremias, or one of the prophets.
>
> He saith unto them, But whom say ye that I am?
>
> And Simon Peter answered and said, Thou art the Christ, the Son of the living God.
>
> Matthew 16:13-16

That Peter answered the critical part of the question certainly reflects his growing knowledge and personal assurance that Jesus of

Nazareth was indeed the Holy Messiah for which Israel had waited so long. It spoke again of his growth in the Gospel and as the senior apostle of Jesus Christ. Mark records that in this small and rather private gathering, Jesus charged them to tell no man of Him, for that knowledge was not yet for the world. Matthew's account of what followed after Peter's dramatic proclamation of Christ's divinity clearly indicates where Peter stood among the apostles and disciples of the Master.

> And Jesus answered and said unto him, Blessed art thou Simon Bar-jona: for flesh and blood hath not revealed it unto thee, but my Father which is in heaven.
>
> And I say also unto thee, that thou art Peter, and upon this rock I will build my Church; and the gates of hell shall not prevail against it.
>
> And I will give unto thee the keys of the kingdom of heaven: and whatsoever thou shalt bind on earth shall be bound in heaven: and whatsoever thou shalt loose on earth shall be loosed in heaven.
>
> *Matthew 16:17-19*

Following Peter's inspired proclamation of His divinity, the Savior found it necessary to explain the harsh realities that awaited Him. Matthew records it thusly.

> From that time forth began Jesus to shew unto his disciples, how that he must go unto Jerusalem, and suffer many things of the elders and chief priests and scribes, and be killed, and be raised again the third day.
>
> *Matthew 16:21*

Although Peter had come to know of Jesus' divine Sonship and His status as the Christ, he did not yet understand the purpose and meaning of the atoning sacrifice and the resurrection of the Savior. Once again, the senior apostle's boldness and ignorance of a critical element in Christ's divine ministry presented Jesus with a teaching moment in Peter's life.

> Then Peter took him, and began to rebuke him, saying, Be it far from thee, Lord: this shall not be unto thee.
>
> *Matthew 16:22*

Matthew probably did not know all that went through Jesus' mind as Peter rebuked the Master. Whatever thoughts Jesus had, He found it necessary to reverse their roles and rebuke Peter.

> But he turned, and said unto Peter, Get thee behind me, Satan: thou art an offence unto me: for thou savourest not the things that be of God, but those that be of men.
>
> *Matthew 16:23*

Christ's words were indeed stern and harsh. Peter, of course, was not Satan, but his rebuke of Christ appears to have been based on a deep misunderstanding at this point in his life about the atonement, and in some ways reflected negatively on Jesus' divine mission. That Peter had no control over the life and death of Christ was not yet clear to the senior apostle and all of his colleagues. Because he thought like a man about life and death, and had the temerity and audacity to question Christ's explanation about His divine mission, a harsh rebuke was indeed required. Clearly the fisherman from Bethsaida needed more instruction and loving counsel, and Peter of course would continue to provide those moments for the Master.

How I wish we had a personal record of these events written by Peter himself. How did he feel after the latest verbal exchange with Christ? Was he hurt? Did it embarrass him? Was he angry? Did he quietly withdraw and ponder his mistake and Christ's words to him? Whatever his feelings and thoughts were, he did not quit.

In the space of a few moments, Peter uttered one of the most important testimonies ever recorded of the Son of God, was declared by Christ to be the holder of the sealing keys and powers of the Holy Priesthood, and rebuked sternly for his well intended but deeply misguided words regarding Christ's forthcoming death. Although his three time denial of knowing Christ on the night of Jesus' trial was undoubtedly Peter's darkest hour, it can probably be said of the above exchange with Christ that it was both one of Peter's finest hours and one of his worst.

At the Mount of Transfiguration, Peter, James, and John were privileged to experience one of the greatest manifestations of divine power recorded in scripture. Among other things, it appears to have been another event designed to educate Peter, James, and John regarding the future of Christ's Church upon the earth, and to introduce them to the ancient prophets who held the various keys of Christ's Gospel. For unknown reasons, John, a participant in this event, did not address or record it in his Gospel. Matthew does not record any other purpose for Christ conferring with Moses and Elias, but we can assume it was vitally important.

The first remarkable event on the Mount was the transfiguration of Jesus, which was witnessed by the three apostles. The Master's face shone as the sun and His raiment or robe became as white as the light, or in Mark's words "his raiment became shining, exceeding white as snow, so as no fuller on earth can white them." *(Mark 9:3)* Whether Christ's transfiguration was solely for their benefit or was necessary to confer with Moses and Elias we are not told, but upon experiencing this auspicious event, Peter spoke to Jesus saying:

> Master, it is good for us to be here: and let us make three tabernacles; one for thee, and one for Moses and one for Elias.
>
> *Mark 9:5*

Once again, Peter was thinking mostly mortal thoughts. Tabernacles were indeed part of Israel's history, but they had no purpose here, as Peter quickly learned. Matthew tells us that

> While he yet spake, behold, a bright cloud overshadowed them: and behold a voice out of the cloud, which said, This is my beloved Son, in whom I am well pleased: hear ye him.
>
> And when the disciples heard it, they fell on their face, and were sore afraid.
>
> And Jesus came and touched them, and said, Arise, and be not afraid.
>
> *Matthew 17:5-7*

This indeed was an august occasion. The three apostles were privileged to hear, as did John the Baptist and Joseph Smith, the Father's statement that Jesus of Nazareth was indeed His Beloved Son. This powerful witness, in combination with Christ's transfiguration and the appearance of Moses and Elias constituted an event of incredible and singular grandeur and importance. Having been directed by the Father to speak, we can assume that Christ used the occasion to instruct the three apostles in matters of truth, doctrine, and Priesthood power in further preparation for their apostolic presidency.

Peter's desire to build three tabernacles was certainly based upon the best of intentions. It was again a sign of his mortal mentality and his desire to do good. Again events of a much higher order overtook the humble fisherman. Added to the previous powerful lessons, Jesus taught Peter that there is a time to build tabernacles and a time to hear the voice of the Father proclaiming Christ's divine Sonship. Jesus' education of Peter concerning the things of God had taken another great step forward. It was, however, not yet complete.

Several other episodes in Christ's efforts to prepare Peter for his great calling and responsibilities to be the earthly leader of the Church after the Savior's ascension into heaven are compressed into the last few days of Christ's mortal life and ministry. That he still needed polishing after several months as Christ's senior apostle is very obvious. His actions in word and deed were not yet under control. Peter and his fellow apostles and disciples were still unprepared for the momentous events that would unfold in the next three days.

Following the conclusion of the final week with the chosen twelve in the upper room, we get the following account from John:

> He riseth from supper, and laid aside his garments; and took a towel, and girded himself.
>
> Then cometh he to Simon Peter: and Peter saith unto him, Lord dost thou wash my feet?
>
> Jesus answered and said unto him, What I do thou knowest not now; but thou shalt know hereafter.
>
> *John 13:4, 6-7*

Then, in vintage form,

> Peter saith unto him, **Thou shalt never wash my feet.** Jesus answered him, If I wash thee not, thou has no part of me.
>
> *John 13:8, (Emphasis added)*

As quickly as Peter had told the Lord that He would never wash his feet, he took a mental leap of great magnitude, and again attempted to tell Jesus what to do.

> Simon Peter, saith unto him, **Lord not my feet only but also my hands and my head.**
>
> *John 13:9, (Emphasis added)*

Having had similar conversations and encounters with Peter several times in the past, one wonders if Christ did not think, "Here we go again." This time Jesus gently reminded the Chief Apostle that:

> He that is washed needeth not save to wash his feet, but is clean every whit: and ye are clean, but not all.
>
> *John 13:10*

What a comfort it must have been to Peter and all of the apostles except Judas Iscariot to hear Christ pronounce them clean except one.

Having finished the Last Supper and completed the ordinance of washing the apostles' feet, Jesus found it necessary to again commune with His Father. The events that lie immediately ahead were bearing heavily on the Son of God. The mortal part of His being was starting to sense the great burden that was His to bear. Jesus knew that He needed strength and support from His Heavenly Father. He took Peter, James, and John with Him to a place in the Garden of Gethsemane where He could express to His Father the feelings that had come upon Him. More critical even than His feelings and fears was the fact that in Gethsemane He would take upon himself the sins of all mankind. The finite mind of man can perhaps understand in a small way Christ's feelings and fears at that hour. However, it cannot fathom or comprehend what would take place as He sweat drops of blood from every pore as He bore the collective sins of all mankind.

We can, perhaps, in this terribly dark and difficult hour of Christ's life understand why He felt the need for support and strength from Peter, James, and John. While they could not stop or change the events that were about to occur in Gethsemane and on Calvary, Jesus apparently hoped they would provide some measure of comfort to Him. Matthew's next verse records one of the most touching passages of scripture ever recorded:

> Then saith he unto them, My soul is exceedingly sorrowful, even unto death: tarry ye here and watch with me.
>
> And he went a little further, and fell on his face, and prayed, saying, O my Father, if it be possible, let this cup pass from me: nevertheless not as I will, but as thou wilt.
>
> *Matthew 26:38-39*

As we know, the will of the Father took precedence over the humble petition of His Beloved Son. To have removed the cup would have thwarted all that had been decreed since the Council in Heaven. The eternal life of man would be lost, his agency destroyed, and Satan handed a victory that would compensate him for all of his past defeats. As Christ knew He would, His Father, rather than removing the cup, strengthened His Son and gave Him the courage and strength to proceed with His trial, His crucifixion and the indescribable agony and pain those events would impose upon Him. Only Jesus knows if the Father came personally to the Garden or spoke verbally or worked through the Holy Ghost. Luke tells us that an angel came and ministered unto Christ. *(Luke 22:43)*

Following His first petition to His Father, Matthew records that Christ walked back to the place where He had left His three apostles. Jesus did not conceal His disappointment:

> And he cometh unto the disciples and findeth them asleep, and saith unto Peter, What, could ye not watch with me one hour?
>
> Watch and pray, that ye enter not into temptation: the spirit indeed is willing, but the flesh is weak.
>
> *Matthew 26:40–41*

Matthew tells us that for a second time Christ went back into the Garden and asked His Father if the cup could pass from Him, stating again that the Father's will and not His be done.

And a second time He returned to find Peter, James, and John asleep. A third time Jesus returned to the Garden to ask His Father about the bitter cup, and obediently stating that He would drink thereof if it was the will of the Father. As on the previous two occasions, the answer was the same. The reasons for His crucifixion had not changed the mind or will of God, despite three humble petitions from His beloved Son. A different Jesus emerged from the third and final petition to His Father. The power of God was upon Him, peace reigned in His soul, and Jesus of Nazareth was finally prepared to die for all mankind and to effect the infinite atonement.

When Christ came out of the Garden for the last time, He once again found His three apostles fast asleep, prompting Him to utter these words to them, and His own declaration that the cup was now His to drink and that He would do the will of the Father.

> Then cometh he to his disciples, and saith unto them, Sleep on now, and take your rest: behold the hour is at hand, and the son of man is betrayed into the hands of sinners.
>
> *Matthew 26:45*

The great story here, of course, is Christ pleading with His Father, not once but thrice, to remove the cup, and the Father's decision to require the atoning sacrifice and brutal crucifixion of His Son. The secondary story is that Peter, James and John had slept through all or most of Christ's agony in the Garden and failed in their small way to give Him the support He had sought from them. And again, Peter was one of those whom Christ chastised. Peter's darkest hour, however, was still ahead of him.

According to Mark's account, sometime between the last supper in the upper room and Christ's departure for the Garden of Gethsemane, there occurred yet another dialogue between Jesus and Peter at the Mount of Olives.

> And Jesus saith unto them, All ye shall be offended because of me this night: for it is written, I will smite the shepherd, and the sheep shall be scattered.
>
> *Mark 14:27*

Peter, ever the first spokesman, contradicted Jesus.

> But Peter said unto him, Although all shall be offended, yet will not I.
>
> And Jesus saith unto him, Verily I say unto thee, That this day even in this night, before the cock crow twice, thou shalt deny me thrice.
>
> But he spake the more vehemently, If I should die with thee, I will not deny thee in any wise. Likewise also said they all.
>
> *Mark 14:29-31*

Peter's bravado, though well intended, was ill spoken. The lessons were not yet fully learned from the water walking episode and Christ's rebuke of Peter for rebuking Him; Peter's bravado would turn to shame and bitter tears before the sun rose over Jerusalem. As always, Jesus knew Peter better than Peter knew himself. Christ's project to prepare Peter, though not complete, was nearing an end.

As Christ emerged from the Garden, Judas, the Chief Priests, and the elders met Him whereupon Judas identified Jesus with his infamous kiss of betrayal. Peter's long and painful night was just getting started. His next act gave Jesus the opportunity to perform a small miracle, to once again chastise Peter and to make a prophetic statement regarding war and violence. John is the only gospel writer to identify Peter as the swordsman.

Then Simon Peter having a sword drew it, and smote the high priest's servant, and cut off his right ear. The servant's name was Malchus.

> Then said Jesus unto Peter, Put up thy sword into the sheath: the cup which my Father hath given me, shall I not drink it?
>
> *John 18:10-11*

Jesus then simply touched the servant's severed ear and it was healed. *(Luke 22:51)*

Thus under very difficult circumstances, Jesus used the occasion to again teach Peter and to counsel the world again regarding violence and war, and to remind His captors that He was submitting willingly.

> Then said Jesus unto him, Put up again thy sword into its place: for all they that take the sword shall perish with the sword.
>
> Thinkest thou that I cannot now pray to my Father, and he shall presently give me more than twelve legions of angels?
>
> *Matthew 26:52-53*

Jesus then quietly and meekly surrendered to those determined to put Him to death. His trial would start later that night. Christ's direct teaching and molding of Peter, while the mortal Messiah, would soon end, to be continued after His resurrection from the grave. Peter's darkest hour would come before the next dawn, and it would be a significant turning point in the chief apostle's life and new ministry.

Jesus' arrest and trial before Annas, Caiaphas, and the Sanhedrin pulled Peter to the fringes of that institution and those events. That he did not go in boldly and openly is recorded by the Gospel writers. But he went nevertheless. By this time in Peter's life, he was quite recognizable. For many months he had traveled, taught and been intimately associated with the Man on trial. Matthew records these terribly painful hours in Peter's life.

> Now Peter sat without in the palace: and a damsel came unto him, saying, Thou also wast with Jesus of Galilee.
>
> But he denied before them all, saying I know not what thou sayest.
>
> And when he was gone out onto the porch, another maid saw him, and said unto them that were there, This fellow was also with Jesus of Nazareth.
>
> And again he denied with an oath, I do not know the man.
>
> And after a while came unto him they that stood by, and said to Peter, Surely thou art one of them: for thy speech bewrayeth thee.
>
> Then began he to curse and to swear saying, I know not the man. And immediately the cock crew.
>
> And Peter remembered the word of Jesus, which said unto him, Before the cock crow, thou shall deny me thrice. And he went out, and wept bitterly.
>
> *Matthew 26: 69-75*

Jesus, of course, knew what Peter had just gone through. Despite everything in Peter's life to this point, Jesus still deeply loved him. It would take more time, more work, and more teaching, but Christ's long, patient, and frequently forceful molding of Peter had brought him to the point where his leadership would be accepted and recognized. None of Christ's apostles or disciples had received such attention from the Master. Perhaps none needed it more than Peter whose accomplishments and service after Christ's death became truly remarkable.

Peter's progress as a man, apostle and earthly leader of Christ's Church for more than thirty years after the Savior's resurrection gives to each of us a marvelous example of how the Gospel of Christ lays out for mankind a pattern of repentance, progress and growth leading to eternal life. Above, I have documented certain events in Peter's life that contributed so positively to his remarkable growth and change. Let me now document what he became as a result of Christ's tutelage and the continued revelation from the Savior as he masterfully led the Church Christ established. Space of course doesn't allow coverage of everything recorded in the Scriptures about this great and wonderful man.

As Senior Apostle Peter took several steps to sustain and build the actual structure and organization of the Church. The first chapter of Acts tells us that under his direction the eleven apostles and other members of the Church gathered in a meeting to choose a new apostle to succeed Judas Iscariot. Under his guidance two men were selected, Joseph called Barsabas who was surnamed Justus and Matthias. After much prayer, the apostles cast lots and Matthias was chosen. Under Peter's inspired leadership the quorum once again had the required twelve members. *(Acts 1:22-26)*

In another inspired move, Peter and the apostles called seven men including Stephen to assist in administering the temporal affairs of the Church, since "It is not reason that we should leave the word of God, and serve tables." *(Acts 6:2-5)* Peter astutely recognized the correct division of labor.

It took only a short time for the formerly unlettered fisherman to become an inspiring orator and advocate for Christ. On the day of Pentecost, amidst the outpouring of the great power of the Holy Ghost, Peter rose and expounded the scriptures and the role of the third member of the Godhead to all assembled. He then admonished them to repent and be baptized. Luke, the author of the early chapters of the Book of Acts tells us that about three thousand souls were baptized on that occasion. Peter had become a great missionary. *(Acts 2)*

On another occasion his divine authority was demonstrated as he entered the temple with his longtime friend and colleague John. In responding to "a certain man lame" who pled for alms at the temple gate, Peter told him that he was monetarily poor but spiritually powerful. "Silver and gold have I none; but such as I have give I thee: In the name of Jesus Christ of Nazareth rise up and walk. And he took him by the right hand, and lifted him up: and immediately his feet and ankle bones received strength." *(Acts 3:2, 6-7)*

Peter performed an act similar to what Christ did with Jairus' daughter and Lazarus. Leading up to this miracle of calling Tabitha back from the dead, he raised Æneas from his sick bed of eight years and cured him of his palsy. Moving on to Joppa he was asked to come to the home of the woman who lived a very Christ-like life and who had died. He had genuine compassion for her and the charitable services and alms she performed for others. The scripture describing this act is very moving. "But Peter put them all forth, and kneeled down, and prayed; and turning him to the body said, Tabitha, arise. And she opened her eyes: and when she saw Peter, she sat up." *(Acts 9:40)* The fisherman who couldn't walk on water raised a dear sister from the dead through the power of God.

As significant as the above experiences were in Peter's growth as the Chief Apostle, the events recorded in the Tenth chapter of Acts reveal something much more far reaching because they affected all of mankind. Cornelius's vision set the stage for Christ's next great act in building His church and teaching Peter anew the principle of obedience. The Apostle was residing at Joppa with Simon a tanner and in response to the inquiry to God by this faithful and devout Centurion of the Italian band, Christ gave Peter one of the great visions and commandments of all time. Not surprisingly Peter's initial response reflected his decades of living strict Jewish dietary laws.

As the vessel descended to the earth containing "All manner of fourfooted beasts of the earth, and wild beasts, and creeping things, and fowls of the air" the voice of the Lord issued a firm command, "Rise, Peter; kill, and eat." Peter's response sounded like a voice from the past, "Not so, Lord; for I have never eaten any thing that is common or unclean. And the voice spake unto him again the second time, What God hath cleansed, that call not thou common." *(Acts 10:11-15)* Although this vision was repeated three times Peter would not learn its full meaning until after his discussions were completed with Cornelius and his extended household. It then became apparent to him, "Peter opened his mouth, and said, Of a truth I perceive that God is no respecter of persons: But in every nation he that feareth him, and worketh righteousness, is accepted with him." *(Acts 10:34-35)* Thus through Peter came the great and marvelous message from the Lord that all peoples are children of God and the Gospel of Jesus Christ would at some point in time be available to every human being who had or will ever dwell upon the earth.

Finally Peter's astounding progress is demonstrated in two short epistles to the early church wherein he showed himself to be a brilliant writer and expounder of eternal truths and principles to members of the primitive church.

Speaking to true believers he stated, "But ye are a chosen generation, a royal priesthood, an holy nation, a peculiar people; that ye should shew forth the praises of him who hath called you out of darkness into his marvellous light." *(1 Peter 2:9)* This description of saints is also applicable to the Church today.

The Chief Apostle also shed great light on those who died or will die without hearing the gospel of salvation noting that Christ "...went and preached unto the spirits in prison" *(1 Peter 3:19)* and "For for this cause was the gospel preached also to them that are dead, that they might be judged according to men in the flesh, but live according to God in the spirit." *(1 Peter 4:6)*

He warned all of us "that no prophecy of the scripture is of any private interpretation," a principle of great importance in a world where the temptation to do so is ever present. *(2 Peter 1:20)*

In another verse Peter counseled each of us to live in such a way as to make our "calling and election sure" in the kingdom of God. *(2 Peter 1:10)*

In a Latter-day revelation Christ reiterated to the world that Peter and his fellow Quorum members, "mine apostles, the Twelve which were with me in my ministry at Jerusalem, shall stand at my right hand at the day of my coming in a pillar of fire, being clothed with robes of righteousness, with crowns upon their heads, in glory even as I am, to judge the whole house of Israel." *(D&C 29:12; see also Matthew 19:28)*

Lastly this diamond in the rough, who Christ loved, taught, molded and trusted, had received from the Master the Melchizedek Priesthood and its vital sealing powers. Peter was sent to earth in 1829 with his colleagues James and John to restore to the Latter-day Church that same authority for the blessing of all mankind.

As noted earlier only a few are called to the Holy Apostleship. All however, are called to be devout and obedient disciples. Many of us have started as humble unlettered fishermen. We can all travel the straight and narrow path using Peter as a beacon and a guide.

I love, respect and deeply admire this great man who has taught us so much about personal growth, strength, courage, faith, perseverance and mostly obedience.

The Incomparable Secretariat

See p. 3

A beach in Barbados. Evidence of the beauty of the Savior's Creation.

See p. 13

El Capitan, Yosemite. A manifestation of the majesty of the Creation.
See p. 14

The birth of Jesus, one of the most important and celebrated events of all time.
See p. 17. *Photo courtesy Del Parson. Used with permission*

"Christ Healing the Paralytic at Capernaum" by Bernhard Rode 1780. A great example of Jesus' love and compassion. See p. 79

A great granddaughter and a grandson. We share with Christ a deep love for little children. See p. 39

The Wolthuis family in 2009 at our 50th wedding anniversary. Our relationships with our families teach us how to love as the Savior does. See p. 108

Jesus loved the little children. See p. 35. *Photo courtesy Del Parson. Used with permission*

Archaeological remains of what is believed to be Peter's House in Capernaum. See p. 79

Mother Teresa and I aboard our C-141 Humanitarioan Mission to Albania. See p. 99

United States Air Force C-5, Ethiopia Relief 1991. See p. 84

Chapter Seven

Christ, A Friend of the Poor and Unfortunate

To walk around and observe, as I have, the pyramids of Egypt, the Great Wall in China, the Acropolis, some of the great cathedrals and castles in Europe, the Panama and Suez Canals, and the American transcontinental railroad connecting point at Promontory, Utah, one stands in awe of man's ancient and medieval construction accomplishments. The brilliant minds that designed these great projects deserve their just due. In both ancient and modern times historians have praised and honored the Czars, the Chinese Emperors, the Pharaohs, the European Royalty and the capitalist kings of America for constructing such magnificent structures.

Unfortunately as we marvel at such incredible accomplishments we tend to forget the uncounted thousands of peasants, serfs and slave laborers who actually built these great projects, many of whom died while giving the world these remarkable masterpieces. In our day we don't often praise and thank the men and women who build our houses and make our plumbing work, or the mechanic who keeps our car running, or the truck driver who delivers our groceries to the super market. I believe that Western Society has adopted a perverted sense of the value and worth of individuals.

Ours is a society where money, position, beauty and talent dictate in large measure a person's success in life. The American media generally, but not always, is controlled by the rich and famous, which in turn uses it to promote the rich and famous, and people of status. This structure is not always bad, but only seldom does it focus on the common man and the people on the low end of the economic, social, and political spectrum. Millions of print pages, television hours, and radio time are spent eulogizing, talking about, and pandering over athletes, musicians, politicians, actors and celebrities. The trash in the lives of some of these people keeps many entertained (a fact which proves it does not take much to entertain some people).

The Jesus I know was a great friend of the poor, the sick, the outcasts and the common people of the world. We have no concise record of His association in the pre-existence with His brothers and sisters. From Adam to Zacharias and John the Baptist, He had extensive associations and dealings with the prophets of the Old Testament and somewhat with the children of Israel. There are few, if any recorded instances, where He, as Jehovah, interacted personally and directly with common people. Christ's three year ministry in the meridian of time, however, was very different. To be sure, His relationship with His apostles and disciples was quite close. In some cases, certain friends, such as Martha, Mary, and Lazarus, were practically family to Him.

It is fair to say that, with only a few exceptions, Jesus did not consort with the upper echelons of His society. His relationships with the Roman political leaders and the Jewish religious hierarchy were almost always confrontational. Not so, however, with the bottom end of Jewish society. He sought out the poor, the sick, and the maimed, and also on occasion allowed them to come to Him. Christ became their friend, healer, provider, and frequently their admirer. When the Master came to the Bethesda pool in Jerusalem, He sought out the crippled man who for 38 years had failed in his effort to be the first into the bubbling waters. *(John 5:4-9)* It also appears that the Master was the only one who noticed the poor widow casting her mite into the temple treasury. It is my firm belief that when He returns in great triumph to the earth, He will quickly establish a close and warm relationship with the downtrodden and the poorest of the poor. It is to such people that this narrative now turns. All are not poor or outcasts, but all provide some valuable insights into their character. These incidents will be reviewed from the perspective of the person with whom Christ interacted and not generally from Christ's perspective as I did with the adulterous woman. They considered, I believe, Jesus to be a dear friend. In only a few instances are we given the names of these incredible people whom Jesus loved and served.

Some people and churches hold the view that Jesus Christ belongs to them exclusively. I have known a few Mormons over the years who believed this false concept. Christ is the Savior of all mankind. He died and atoned for the sins of every human being who has or will come to this earth in mortality. The saving and exalting ordinances of Christ's Gospel are, or will be, offered to every one of God's children who kept their first estate. The only claim to exclusiveness regarding the Gospel of Christ is the fact that the Priesthood and the administration of the saving and exalting ordinances do reside only in The Church of Jesus Christ of Latter-day Saints. This simply means that the way is strait and the gate is narrow leading to the respective degrees of glory. The way, however, is never blocked and travel on the road to eternal life can be freely accessed by anyone who wishes to obediently walk that road. Even more important is the great reality that the gate is never locked to anyone who wishes to enter through it, provided they meet Christ's standards and requirements for entry.

Based on the above criteria, Jesus is the Savior of Mormons, Jews, Catholics, Muslims, Buddhists, Caucasians, Africans, Asians, Indians, Arabians, and all other inhabitants of this earth. *(1 Peter 1:17-19)*

Peter taught that God is no respecter of persons, having learned that lesson very graphically when Christ presented to him the vision which informed the Senior Apostle that he must not consider anything unclean that the Father and the Son had declared clean. *(Acts 10-11)*

Christ is even the Redeemer of every evil genius, including Adolf Hitler, Josef Stalin, Mao Tse-tung, Pol Pot, Genghis Khan, Jack the Ripper, and every cold blooded murderer and thug who ever walked the earth. Some or all of these are probably Sons of Perdition, having served as vicious and brutal servants of Satan and his lieutenants.

It has been my privilege to observe and work with a wide range of people, customs, cultures, languages, and races around the world. While

I could not understand Russian, Arabic, French, Croatian, Spanish, or Mongolian, I knew that Jesus did. My initial, and admittedly limited, view of the world and its people began to broaden in 1955 as a missionary in the Netherlands, and further when our small family moved to Virginia in 1962 for me to attend graduate school. At the Johns Hopkins School of Advanced International Studies I became close friends with a fine young Jewish student from the Bronx and a most interesting professor from Bangkok. I met numerous students who had traveled and studied abroad and a few pompous students from Ivy League schools. For thirty-two years it was my privilege and blessing to become acquainted with remarkable people from several nationalities and backgrounds in America's capital.

While this time was crucial to broadening my point of view, there were several events in my life that brought this broadening process to the point where I gained a greater understanding that all men and women are God's children, my spiritual brothers and sisters, and recipients of Christ's divine atonement.

In 1971, while serving as Bishop of the Arlington Ward in Northern Virginia, a young African-American lady moved into the ward. She had recently been baptized in another ward and sought the love and fellowship of the Saints in Arlington. This young woman had great faith and, as we soon learned, an incredible singing voice. She was warmly accepted by most of the congregation. Our ward music director came to me one day and suggested that Sister Jackson sing in Sacrament Meeting. I accepted her proposal, but I was in no way prepared for Sister Jackson's music when it was presented.

Nathleen stood at the pulpit, a lone solitary black woman in an all white ward. Without piano or organ accompaniment, she sang all seven verses of "A Poor Wayfaring Man of Grief" in a voice that only an angel might possess. It was a defining moment in my life and for many people in that ward. Only a few times in my Church life has a meeting been so spiritual and moving. Silence, awe, and respect came over the congregation. It was confirmed to me that Sister Jackson was indeed worthy of all the covenants and ordinances I treasured, and in the Lord's time she would receive the full blessings of the restored gospel. Carolyn and I came to love and respect this remarkable lady.

In the following months I had occasion to visit with her about the Priesthood. The only reassurance I could give, as her Bishop, was that someday it would be given to all of God's children with the attendant blessings.

In 1978, when President Kimball, the First Presidency, and the Quorum of the Twelve presented to the Church the revelation that all worthy males could receive the priesthood, I had a High Council assignment in the Oakton Ward in Virginia. I can still remember stating that the Lord had now made it very clear to the membership of the Church that every member—black, white or brown—was equal in this Church and that all worthy male members, regardless of race, color or ethnic background, were eligible to hold the priesthood, enter the temple and marry anyone who met temple requirements. By that time Nathleen had moved from our ward and stake. I trust that great revelation was a remarkable blessing and joy to her.

Another defining moment affecting my view of other people started in 1984 when I organized and began to administer the Department of Defense Humanitarian Assistance Program. For the first couple of years, our major focus was assisting the Afghan Mujahidin who were struggling to drive the occupying Russians out of their country.

My small staff and I worked directly with the United States Agency for International Development office in Islamabad, Pakistan. That office channeled our excess non-lethal assistance through the Pakistan Army which moved it into Afghanistan. The USAID contact within the Army was Brigadier General Raza, whom I was not permitted to meet for several months. Then one day in late 1984, I was taken to a meeting where Raza and the civilian heads of the seven Afghan political parties were present. Our relationship started off cool, slow and quite guarded. Over the months, however, it warmed considerably and by 1993 when I left DOD, Raza, who was a devout Muslim, and many of his staff had become close friends. On one occasion I brought General Raza and some of his staff to Washington D.C. and introduced them to key State and DOD officials and several supporters in the Congress. In our home, at quiet dinners in Islamabad and

Peshawar, and during the long C-5 and C-141 flights from Pakistan to Andrews Air Force Base, we often talked about Islam, Christianity, eternal questions and the central roles of Mohammed in Islam and Christ in Christianity. General Raza, like Nathleen Jackson and scores of wonderful people since then, taught me important lessons about race, ethnicity and the fact that we are all sons and daughters of God. The Jesus I know is their Savior, as He is mine.

The Savior's interaction with a Samaritan who the Jews despised gives evidence that he was no respecter of persons.

The Samaritan Woman

Jesus Christ was and is the greatest champion of women the world has ever known, despite some modern views to the contrary. His dialogue with the Samaritan woman at Jacob's well recorded in considerable detail by John is proof of that. It is indeed a very interesting and revealing account of the woman who is nameless.

As the conversation unfolded with Christ, she immediately demonstrated that she was no wallflower or introvert. She had a quick mind and showed no fear in calling to Jesus' attention the fact that Jews usually avoided any "dealings" with Samaritans. When the Master kindly offered to give her the gift of "living water" she had the temerity to remind Him that He had no vessel of any kind which He could use to draw water from the well, and that Jacob had dug the well very deep. The lady then boldly asked the Jew with whom she was carrying on this dialogue if He were greater than Jacob. Jesus proceeded to explain that His gift of water was the gift of everlasting life. Her approach then quickly changed to a simple request for the living water, based not on the principle and gift of eternal life, but on the hope that she would no longer thirst, and be spared the task of frequently having to draw water at the well.

It would be most interesting to have Jesus' inner thoughts as He talked to this woman. We can assume based on subsequent events in the next few hours and days that she made quite an impression on Him. Jesus, of course, had not completed His dialogue with her. Being omniscient like His Father, He could have told her that He knew precisely about her marital status and her entire life for that matter, but He chose a different course which tested both her candor and her basic honesty. In fairness to her it must be conceded that she passed the test, but just barely. After Christ suggested she go call her husband, the woman carefully answered, "I have no husband," which was technically correct. She had in fact had five husbands whose status or whereabouts we are not told. At that time this woman of Samaria was involved with a sixth man who was not her actual husband. Thus, her answer that she had no husband, though guarded and not fully revealing, was still basically true.

The woman's boldness and audacity quickly changed to believing acceptance of Christ as a Jew, a prophet and the source of living water. Her spirit was quickly transformed and deeply touched. In a marvelous one on one with Jesus Christ she became a believer, a disciple, and a witness to the people of Samaria.

> The woman saith unto him, I know that Messias cometh, which is called Christ: when he is come, he will tell us all things.
>
> Jesus saith unto her, I that speak unto thee am *he.*
>
> *John 4: 25-26*

She obviously knew the scriptures and we must be impressed that she referred to the Messiah as Christ. Upon hearing, and accepting Jesus' statement that He was the Messiah, this remarkable Samaritan woman then went back into the city and told others that she had found the Christ. Numerous people came, and after some interaction with this Jew from Nazareth, they requested Jesus to tarry in Samaria for two more days. According to John, many believed and accepted Him as the Savior of the world.

As always, Jesus was in complete charge of the episode, but we must give the woman considerable credit. She demonstrated much boldness, knowledge of the coming Messiah, and the faith, courage and intellectual honesty to accept Jesus as the Savior of Mankind. She had the rare privilege of looking Him in the eye and hearing with her own ears His profound statement that He was indeed the long awaited Messiah.

We know nothing more about this most interesting lady. Whether she married the man with whom she was involved or whether she remained a devoted and faithful disciple is currently unknown to us. What we do know is that she was privileged to be one of the first to have the Gospel of Christ taught to someone other than the Jews. Hopefully her life from that day forward was one of joy, faith, and endurance in her first hand knowledge and association with the Son of God.

A Believing Nobleman

Our next event involves a man whose son lay near death. It is recorded only in the fourth chapter of John. His status is described as a "nobleman" who obviously had some wealth and stature in Capernaum. We can assume that he had heard of Jesus and His miracles, and being deeply fearful for the life of his dying son, sought out the Master requesting that He come down to Capernaum and heal the child. We learn at least four important lessons from this man. Obviously he had considerable faith, but probably not enough, since Jesus found it necessary to remind him that "Except ye see signs and wonders, ye will not believe." *(John 4:48)* This mild rebuke by Christ, however, did not deter him from his desperate purpose of asking the Savior to come.

The nameless nobleman then demonstrated two other virtues or characteristics which Jesus quickly honored. It was obvious that he dearly loved his dying son and despite Christ's reminder to him of his need for signs, he did not back off. Showing respect for Christ, he uttered a plea of desperation, "Sir, come down ere my child die." This touched Jesus who then performed a great miracle from afar. How He drove the fever from the boy we are not told. For the Master it was simply an exercise of divine power and higher law as yet not fully understood by man.

The next brief statement by Jesus to the nobleman is most revealing of his character. "Go thy way; thy son liveth." *(John 4:50)* John tells us that the man believed. There was no rejoinder to Christ's admonition to "Go thy way." No argument, no doubt, no hesitation. By now, he had sufficient faith that he "believed" the Master. As he traveled the road back to his home, he almost certainly had mixed feelings, but belief and faith in Christ's words undoubtedly dominated his thoughts.

As he neared Capernaum, he was met by servants who informed him that his son lived and was well, and that at the seventh hour yesterday he was cured. This gift of continued life and good health for his son turned the nobleman and his household into devout believers in Christ. He teaches all readers of John's account regarding this moving encounter with Jesus, important lessons in faith, love, persistence and obedience.

The Healed Leper Who Talked Too Much

Three Gospel writers record the account of Jesus healing a leper who demonstrated great faith, experienced incredible joy, and caused Jesus' notoriety to increase considerably, all within a few hours or perhaps days.

An understanding reader, especially anyone who has been cured of a serious illness or relieved of a heavy personal burden, can sympathize with this poor man. It is my belief that while he caused problems for Christ by his failure to heed the Savior's warning not to publicize his healing, I'm quite certain the Savior understood and was forgiving toward him.

Leprosy was a hideous disease, which in some cases eventually destroyed its victim. The Bible Dictionary notes that even Moses, his sister Miriam, Naaman and King Uzziah were at one time afflicted with the dread disease. In most cases, lepers were segregated from society because the disease was contagious, and they were considered unclean.

The man's identity is left out of the account and the Galilean town where the miracle occurred is not specified. For some reason, however, he was free to seek out Jesus. Mark tells us:

> And there came a leper to him, beseeching him, and saying unto him, If thou wilt, thou canst make me clean.
>
> *Mark 1:40*

Outcast, shunned, desperate, poor, and without hope —but not without faith— was this son of God and spiritual brother of Jesus. His straightforward expression of faith in Christ's healing powers and a plea for relief touched the Master. He was, of course, known to Christ who knew of his past, his life, and suffering, just as He knew about the five husbands of the Samaritan woman. His suffering and expressive plea and conviction of Christ's healing power moved the Master to respond as the man requested. Mark writes:

> And Jesus, moved with compassion, put forth *his* hand and touched him, and saith unto him, I will; be thou clean.
>
> And as soon as he had spoken, immediately the leprosy departed from him, and he was cleansed.
>
> *Mark 1:41-42*

The man had passed the test of faith and was fully healed. By the touch of the Master's hand, his skin was now clean and his status as a social outcast was suddenly changed. None of the Gospel writers record him as saying anything to Christ, but we can assume he was ecstatic, and happy beyond description. Christ understood his personality and emotions. Faithful and healed, the Master then imposed a final test which the man failed. The Savior charged him to "say nothing to any man" and to meet the requirements of presenting himself to the priest and to make the cleansing offering which Moses commanded. *(Mark 1:44)*

We are not told if he went to the priest or made the necessary offering. What we do know is that he talked much and began to "blaze abroad the matter." *(Mark 1:45)* I have frequently pondered Christ's charge to this man to remain silent, since most of the Master's miracles carried no such condition of secrecy. In this case, the man's healing would sooner or later become known to others. We can safely conclude, therefore, that Jesus, knowing him intimately, felt this was a test the former leper must face. This healing miracle would affect Christ's itinerary and agenda in Galilee.

The Jesus I know certainly forgave him and understood his unbridled and uncontrolled joy concerning his new found health. We, as mortals, certainly owe him understanding. Could we keep secret a miracle of this magnitude? We must respect his great faith and share his joy in being liberated from one of the worst diseases of his time. He was able to return to his family, to work and to move freely within Jewish society. This man will answer to Christ for his failure to be quiet, but somehow, I believe the same compassion Christ showed when He healed him was exercised when the two of them discussed his failure to refrain from telling others.

The Centurion and his Servant

The event of the Centurion and his servant also occurred in Capernaum, and must be classified as one which touched Jesus deeply. Although Matthew and Luke record the Centurion's actions somewhat differently, the central theme is the same. It will be helpful to get a deeper understanding of this remarkable man.

The Centurion was almost certainly a Roman by virtue of his command of soldiers. That he was a man of considerable wealth is noted by Luke when he tells us that the servants, in their effort to convince Jesus to come and heal the servant affected with palsy, reminded the Master that the Centurion "loveth our nation and he hath built us a synagogue." *(Luke 7:5)* Whether the servants or the Centurion conferred with Jesus is not the central theme of the miracle. The clear and humble petition to the Master is, and it has multiple threads.

The Centurion loved his servant dearly, which is a great credit to him as a man and human being. He teaches us that those who serve under others, or under ourselves, have great worth and despite their subservient status are worthy of respect, love and personal concern. For whatever reason a person is a subordinate or slave or underling, the Centurion teaches us that they are equal before God in this life. Pride, pomposity, and vain glory were apparently not part of the Centurion's makeup.

Matthew records one of the great lessons of faith and humility recorded in scripture, which is worth being restated. Pursuant to his plea,

> Jesus saith unto him, I will come and heal him.
>
> The centurion answered and said, Lord, I am not worthy that thou shouldest come under my roof: but speak the word only, and my servant shall be healed.
>
> *Matthew 8: 7-8*

With these words this powerful but humble man had succeeded in impressing and touching the Master.

> When Jesus heard it, he marvelled, and said to them that followed, Verily I say unto you, I have not found so great faith, no, not in Israel.
>
> *Matthew 8:10*

My first introduction to serious human suffering occurred in Hue, South Viet Nam, in 1976. What doctors, nurses, corpsmen and countless other caregivers had experienced from time immemorial had not been part of my life. Like so many Americans in the second half of the 20th Century, I had been spared the anguish and trauma of dealing with serious injury, war, disease and suffering. Those who served and fought in World Wars I and II, Korea, Vietnam, Iraq, and Afghanistan were, of course, not spared what I had missed. Christ helped me deal with it.

President Ford created a U.S. Congress Delegation to go to Vietnam and assess continued American appropriations for the South Vietnam Government. I was part of that team as the White House representative, and a small contingent of us made a brief side trip to Hue, near the border with North Vietnam. Our three man delegation, Senator Dewey Bartlett from Oklahoma, Congressman John Murtha from Pennsylvania and myself, was taken to a small hospital which primarily treated children. I was unprepared for what I saw.

In that hospital, which measured about 30' by 70', were several boys and girls ranging from one year to their mid-teens. Some were missing an arm, a leg, or multiple limbs. A couple had their heads heavily bandaged because part of their face or skull had been blown off by a bomb, mortar fire, or land mine. Others were wrapped extensively with bandages to cover the painful burns caused by napalm and other incendiary weapons. My heart sunk and my soul grieved as I walked from bed to bed with the Senator and Congressman. My first reaction was a feeling of sheer helplessness. As I recovered mildly from that emotion, I was graphically taught two other great lessons of life. First, I began to appreciate in a small way the divine compassion which the Vietnamese doctors and nurses in the hospital had for those precious, guiltless victims. The second was the touching lesson I learned from some of these children. Despite their condition and misery, several managed to smile as we walked by their bed, or gently touched their soft cheek or small hand. Their eyes seemed to say things that their mouths could not speak. My helpless reaction was to stand amazed at their resiliency, and to hope that somehow life would be kind to each one. In the years ahead, I visited numerous hospitals and refugee camps treating and caring for victims of war and natural disasters. During that very moving visit in Hue, I had no inkling that eight years later I would be in a position to assist, in a small way, similar victims around the world. The impressions of those kids were forever etched in my mind, but I was guilty of a common human characteristic: in some ways I was anxious to leave the hospital, so I would not have to confront the reality of those children. However, it was very clear to me that Christ loved each one of those children very much, and would not have shared in my human failings. I wished deeply that He could be there and take each one by the hand and restore a limb or heal the burns or take away the pain and sorrow.

I shall not write extensively about other children and adults I have seen, but I do want to mention a few in passing.

The young beggar boy in Minsk whose face was full of scabs and scars from causes unknown to me.

The gypsy women I have seen all over Europe sitting on hard dirty cement, frequently with a small child in their arms or nursing at their breasts. Without question, they are professional beggars, but beggars nonetheless.

A beautiful stately Cambodian widow and her equally beautiful young daughters sitting in a field outside a refugee camp in Thailand waiting to be processed and admitted to the camp. All of her possessions were rolled up in some old rags. She had lost much in life, including her husband, but as she sat there in the weeds, she had enough pride and self respect that she was combing her own and her two young daughters' hair.

Many of us have seen the beggar, in the large and small cities all over the world. These beggars tug at our heartstrings. Sometimes our response is to give a small sum of money, and other times our hearts are hardened. Each person who can respond to the beggar's outstretched hand must answer that question himself or herself. What we cannot dismiss is Christ's mandate in Matthew:

> For I was an hungred, and ye gave me meat: I was thirsty, and ye gave me drink: I was a stranger, and ye took me in:
>
> Naked, and ye clothed me: I was sick, and ye visited me: I was in prison, and ye came unto me.
>
> Then shall the righteous answer him, saying, Lord, when saw we thee an hungred, and fed thee? or thirsty, and gave thee drink?
>
> When saw we thee a stranger, and took thee in? or naked, and clothed thee?
>
> Or when saw we thee sick, or in prison, and came unto thee?
>
> And the King shall answer and say unto them, Verily I say unto you, Inasmuch as ye have done it unto one of the least of these my brethren, ye have done it unto me.
>
> *Matthew 25:35-40*

Christ's answer tells us several things of great importance. First, the least of these, the hungry, the poor, and the downtrodden are very precious to the Savior. Secondly, the responsibility to care for and assist them is placed upon those who have the means to do so. A dollar or a quarter given to a beggar, a pair of shoes donated to the Deseret Industries or Goodwill, and a visit to a sick friend are in fact gifts and service to the Master Himself.

In the nearly twelve years I spent in the humanitarian business at the Department of Defense and as an LDS humanitarian missionary with my wife in Eastern Europe and the Middle East, I learned the true meaning of Christ's statement in verse 40.

I estimate that in those dozen years the two programs I was involved in, one secular and the other religious, donated over $1.5 billion in food, clothing and other necessary goods to countless recipients, most of whom were in desperate need. At no time nor on any occasion did I observe an angel from Heaven creating the goods or managing the delivery and distribution of those necessities of life. That reality confirmed Christ's mandate to me. We who are able and willing are his humanitarian agents. We, not angels, manufacture, cook, assemble, deliver and in a kind and loving way present to His friends and victims, the loaf of bread, medicine, the coat, the clean water and the kindness of a visit.

The Paralytic Healed

The miracle of the healed paralytic is one of great consequence for all involved: for the reader, for Jesus, and for the healed paralytic and the valiant and tenacious friends who brought the man to the house where Jesus was teaching. We again do not know his name or age and very little about his status, but some speculative background will be helpful in gaining an appreciation for this man and his friends.

This man's paralysis was obviously very incapacitating; it is most probable that he was unable to use his legs because he appeared to be permanently bedridden. There was clearly no medical treatment that could help him. We do not know if he was a father, a cherished son, or an old man. We can safely assume that he was poor, had little or no hope for a full and active life, and looked darkly at his life. But he had some things that were more valuable than wealth, status, or the then defined luxuries of life. This unfortunate soul had two of life's greatest possessions: a rare combination of determination, hope and faith; and friends who were willing to help him.

Where and when he learned of Jesus is not recorded by any of the Gospel writers, but learn he did, and what he heard and knew caused the dual spark of faith and hope in his soul to ignite into a plan of bold action.

If he could somehow find this man Jesus and personally ask that He exercise His great healing power, then he could walk and be a whole man. Word somehow reached him that Jesus of Nazareth was in a house in the vicinity teaching a group of people. Alfred Edersheim is of the view that the crowd was assembled in the Apostle Peter's house, although James E. Talmadge and the authors of the synoptic Gospels do not go so far as to establish the location as Peter's residence.*

Somewhere nearby a righteous and worthwhile conspiracy was plotted. The paralytic and some of his friends concluded that they must quickly go to the house where Jesus was. Through the narrow streets they carried the paralytic to the identified location, but as they reached the place, they found a crowd so large that access to Jesus through the regular entrances was impossible. However these guys wouldn't give up. Knowing that Jesus was inside, perhaps in a court yard, one or all of them got the brilliant idea to conduct a descent through the roof. Up a stairway they went and made their way to a location on the roof above where Jesus was teaching. The omniscient Master certainly knew what they were doing. At the point when they started to remove the roof materials, their operation became obvious. Once the roof opening was sufficiently large, the friends carefully lowered this man of great faith and considerable nerve down to the floor right at the feet of Jesus. We have no recorded instance in scripture where Jesus smiled or laughed. Wept yes, but if there was a time when the Master might have smiled because of someone's faith and daring, this was it. No record of permission being asked, no record of who later repaired the owner's roof,

---

*Alfred Edersheim, *The Life and Times of Jesus the Messiah*, Hendrickson Publishers, USA, 1997, pp 345-350; James E. Talmage, *Jesus the Christ*, Deseret Book Company, Salt Lake City, 1955, pp 190-193

and only a brief comment regarding the crowd's reaction.

As usual, Christ had full command of the situation. Luke tells us, "And when he saw their faith, he said unto him, Man, thy sins are forgiven thee." *(Luke 5:20)*

Jesus then completed the healing process and told the man,

> I say unto thee, Arise, and take up thy bed, and go thy way into thine house.
>
> And immediately he arose, took up the bed, and went forth before them all; insomuch that they were all amazed, and glorified God, saying, We never saw it on this fashion.
>
> *Mark 2:11-12*

You can be sure they had never seen it in this fashion. The man's sins were forgiven, though we should not assume that his sins were the cause of his paralysis. He stood up, something he had not done for years or perhaps even for his entire life, and picked up his ramshackle bed and steadily walked out through the crowd. I really wonder if there was perhaps the trace of a smile on his face as he left the house. His friends, who probably watched the brief but incredible miracle from the roof, may or may not have repaired the opening. We can assume they hastily made their way down to the doorway to embrace their friend.

As he walked home carrying his bed, or perhaps he flung it aside somewhere along the way, the healed paralytic must have felt tremendous gratitude to Jesus and his friends. Again, like the adulterous woman, the nine unthanking lepers and the widow of Nain, this remarkable man fades instantly from the pages of scriptural history. But like so many others, he and his friends teach us some meaningful lessons. Innovative and daring action allowed them to overcome a huge blockade at the door of the house. Their combined faith was so strong that Jesus acted upon the man's request immediately. The paralytic was one of only a few people who had the opportunity to actually lie at the Master's feet and was privileged to hear from the Son of God that his sins were forgiven. This exercise of divine power was followed by the quiet, but firm command to take up his bed and walk.

Their bold act caused Jesus some problems with the scribes and Pharisees, but the confrontation over Christ's authority and power to forgive sins was a confrontation which Christ chose to initiate.

The Woman With Blood Disease

This remarkable healing by Jesus of a woman with an "issue of blood twelve years" is most unique because of the way it occurred. *(Matthew 9:20)* Jesus was enroute to the home of Jairus, a ruler in the synagogue who had in great faith plead with Jesus to come and lay His hands on his daughter who was near death. Mark tells us that many people thronged Jesus as He made His way to the young girl's home.

In the crowd was this woman who had been ill for a dozen years with an incurable blood disease that had sapped her physically and had caused her to spend all of her resources on physicians who could not heal her. Again her name is not mentioned, but she has become a legend in holy writ because of her faith. Her disease was growing worse; she was destitute and had no hope for relief at the hand of man. The synoptic Gospel writers are unanimous in noting that she was behind Jesus as He passed through the heavy throng. Luke states that she touched the "border" of His garment. *(Luke 8:44)* Matthew says she touched the "hem" thereof. *(Matthew 9:20)* Those accounts raise the question: was she was so ill that she was sitting or lying on the ground as Jesus passed? Her body was racked with disease, but her mind and spirit were active, strong and driven by the absolute faith and conviction that "If I may but touch his garment, I shall be whole." *Matthew 9:21*

She felt no need to converse with the Master. She made no request directly to Him, as others had, that He say the word or lay His hands on her to drive the disease from her body. She apparently had no friends or family present to assist her. As the great Healing Physician approached, she was terribly alone and just another person in the great throng. As Jesus passed by her, she reached out her hand and succeeded in her plan to touch His robe. Two remarkable physical phenomena then occurred because of her great act of faith. Mark describes them in these words:

> And straightway the fountain of her blood was dried up; and she felt in her body that she was healed of that plague.
> And Jesus, immediately knowing in himself that virtue had gone out of him, turned him about in the press, and said, Who touched my clothes?
>
> *Mark 5:29-30*

Luke's account is even more precise.

> And Jesus said, Somebody hath touched me: for I perceive that virtue is gone out of me.
>
> *Luke 8:46*

We shall resist the temptation to comment on the apostles' efforts to brush aside Christ's perceptions, and their feeble efforts at crowd control. The departure of virtue from Christ's body raises several questions that we cannot definitively answer. This is a unique situation where we are told that departing virtue from Christ's body was part of the healing process. We do know that he used various other means including wet clay, a spoken word from afar, a simple touch and laying His hands on the person.

The three Gospel accounts seem to infer that Christ was not aware of the woman but that is probably an unreal assumption. That He knew she was there, the desires of her heart, and the great faith that underscored her simple plan to touch His garment are not illogical conclusions. I believe He chose to let the woman complete her plan and exercise the incredible faith that drove it.

Her carefully laid plans to fade back into the throng and remain anonymous failed. Although I am convinced that Jesus knew who she was, He took a moment before proceeding on to Jairus' house to bless her life even further. Mark tells us that:

And he looked around about to see her that had done this thing.

But the woman fearing and trembling, knowing what was done in her, came and fell down before him, and told him all the truth.

> And he said unto her, Daughter, thy faith hath made thee whole; go in peace, and be whole of thy plague.
>
> *Mark 5:32-34*

She went her way in good health, where, we do not know, but she went with the unforgettable privilege of having heard from the Holy Messiah a simple compliment regarding her remarkable faith and the never-to-be-forgotten privilege of beholding His countenance and the gaze of His kind and all-seeing eyes. This marvelous lady's joy and faith in being healed probably lasted for the rest of her mortal life. We can assume that she was a devout disciple and an obedient soul. We owe her a great debt. To match her faith, her humility and strong desire to avoid the spotlight and notoriety are lessons of human conduct each one of us should pursue.

One of my most frustrating experiences was in Ethiopia in 1991. As the administrator of the Department of Defense (DOD) humanitarian excess property program, I got a large windfall of Meals Ready to Eat (MRE's) from the U.S. Military in Saudi Arabia left over from the first Gulf War. Because of the relative proximity of Dhahran, Saudi Arabia, to Ethiopia, we offered to donate large quantities of these MRE's to the Government of Ethiopia for the purpose of feeding the transient refugees and soldiers who were moving throughout the country back to their regional homelands without food.

Ground transportation to Addis Ababa was not an option because of the distance and the Red Sea, so we offered to deliver the MRE's by C-5 airlift. After making numerous flights over several weeks time, the airport operators in Addis notified the American Embassy that we owed them approximately $500,000 in landing and use fees for the deliveries, and that future flights would be charged roughly $10,000 each to cover these fees. Our State Department people told them that the U.S. Government did not pay for the privilege of donating humanitarian supplies and transporting them without cost to the receiving government. It cost my program $5,000 an hour to use a C-5 aircraft and the round trip took several hours in flying time. With an attitude that was indeed mind boggling, the airport officials rejected our position: "You must pay or you cannot land." They were in fact saying, "To hell with our hungry refugees, pay up or no landing." In what was one of the most agonizing decisions we ever had to make in the U.S. Government regarding humanitarian relief during my tenure at DOD, we regretfully informed the Ethiopian Government that the flights would be terminated.

An experience quite different from the Ethiopian Government's shortsightedness and callousness occurred with wounded Mujahidin and civilian victims of the war in Afghanistan during the 1980's. As the conflict there ground on, combat casualties mounted. The Mujahidin rudimentary medical system could not effectively take care of the mounting numbers, especially as the Soviets intensified their air attacks. The USAID people in Islamabad and representatives from the International Organization on Migration (IOM) came to me in 1987 and asked if it would be possible to airlift wounded Afghans to the U.S. and Europe for medical care. At the time our DOD program was flying one C-141 and one C-5 aircraft into Islamabad each month. The C-141 was the U.S. Air Force's medical evacuation aircraft and it was returning to the continental United States empty, so the fit was good. The C-5 has a 73-seat troop passenger compartment in the upper rear portion of the fuselage. I had no problem in selling the idea to my boss, the Assistant Secretary of Defense, and the Deputy Secretary of Defense.

After a few fits and starts, the Air Force and my office decided to use the C-141 as the aircraft for patients going to cities in Europe and the United States. Once the treatment was completed, we flew these brave Afghans back to Islamabad in the C-5's. From 1987 until January 1993, when I was forced to retire by newly elected Bill Clinton and left the DOD program, we had brought 1,450 people to the U.S. and Europe for advanced medical care.

The Good Samaritan aspect of the story was that each Afghan was treated pro-bono by doctors and hospitals in the U.S. In Europe, for the most part, they were treated in national health care system hospitals where the cost was paid by the respective governments.

I flew on many of these flights, frequently with a soldier who had a new prosthesis, or a child whose head was now free of shrapnel. The program did not remove the sting of war, but for those who were its victims, it sometimes meant the difference between life and death or the ability to function as a semi-normal human being. It was a marvelous humanitarian effort made successful by DOD's aircraft, the administration, and organizational expertise of IOM, the health screening of various private volunteer organizations in Peshawar, Pakistan, and especially by the numerous doctors, nurses and hospital administrators in America and Europe who provided the excellent medical care.

The Canaanite Woman

Another of Christ's miraculous healings dealt with a woman from Canaan and her daughter. *(Matthew 15:22)* Mark states that she "was a Greek, a Syrophenician by nation." *(Mark 7:26)* This made her a gentile. Her name is not given by either writer, both of whom probably never knew it.

Her daughter was grievously vexed with a devil, and having heard of Jesus' miracles, she found him and plead with the Master to cast the devil from her daughter whom she obviously loved dearly.

This woman possessed a significant amount of persistence, and like most others whom Jesus helped, a great deal of faith. When Jesus ignored her, on the premise that she was not of the House of Israel, she refused to give up. Jesus' reply was both a literal definition of His Father's assignment to come first to the House of Israel, and a test of the woman.

> But he answered and said, I am not sent but unto the lost sheep of the house of Israel.
>
> Then came she and worshipped him, saying, Lord, help me.
>
> But he answered and said, It is not meet to take the children's bread, and to cast it to dogs.
>
> *Matthew 15:24-26*

Her answer to Christ's reference about casting Israel's bread, or the Gospel to Gentile people, caused her to pass the test Christ had imposed upon her.

> And she said, Truth, Lord: yet the dogs eat of the crumbs which fall from their masters' table.
>
> *Matthew 15: 27*

This reply shows us that her mind was quick, that she was not going to back down and quite possibly had some inkling based on her great faith that one day the non Jews, or the Gentiles, would also receive the bread of life initially reserved for the House of Israel.

Underlying her remarkable dialogue with the Redeemer of the World who was the source of the living water, is her persistence, her remarkable faith and her devotion to and love for her daughter.

We should not read into this episode any intended or actual rudeness or disrespect on the part of Jesus for the woman. Like so many others who came pleading for help, He tested her. He had already shared some aspects of His glorious gospel with the woman and people of Samaria, and would, in not too many months hence, give Peter the charge to take the Gospel to all of the world. He sternly often repeated the statement to the senior apostle that no man should treat any people or nation unclean that God had ordained to receive the gospel. *(Acts 10:9-15)* To Paul, a similar calling would be given. *(Acts 9:15)* This woman touched Jesus, and His next statement to her was much different than when He first ignored her and then proclaimed that Israel came first.

> Then Jesus answered and said unto her, O woman, great is thy faith: be it unto thee even as thou wilt. And her daughter was made whole from that very hour.
>
> *Matthew 15:28*

Mark tells us that when she returned to her home, the devil, just as Christ promised, had departed from her daughter. She is another who teaches us never to give up; to argue firmly, but politely, our cause when we are convinced that it is just and true, and to understand where we fit in the eternal scheme of things.

Ten Lepers: A Lesson in Gratitude

In our current world of insatiable greed and gross materialism, often described as a "Me Generation," the healing of the ten lepers by the Master teaches us a significant lesson in gratitude. From this episode recorded only by Luke, we learn a second great lesson from Jesus himself: a sincere expression of gratitude to the giver of a blessing or a precious gift is deeply appreciated. Enroute to Jerusalem, Jesus passed through Galilee and Samaria. As He entered an unidentified village, ten men afflicted with leprosy, standing afar off "lifted up their voices and said, Jesus Master, have mercy on us." (*Luke 17:13-14*)

Christ's response was somewhat different than they expected. Unlike the single leper Jesus had cured by a simple touch of His hand, He instructed these men to show themselves unto the priest. Their faith was sufficient enough that they obeyed the Master's command, and even as they went they were healed. Their happiness and joy were undoubtedly great. Their bodies were now disease free and societal intercourse was again possible. A productive life was opened unto each man whose cup was indeed running over, and whose joy was exceedingly full. But only one remembered the giver of the gift.

> And one of them, when he saw that he was healed, turned back, and with a loud voice glorified God,
> And fell down on *his* face at his feet, giving him thanks: and he was a Samaritan.
>
> *Luke 17:15-16*

Jesus clearly appreciated this man's thoughtful, humble, and obviously loud expression of gratitude. What a great credit it was to this Samaritan leper that even in the hour of his indescribable happiness and relief, his character was such that he returned to express deep gratitude to the great healer and his benefactor.

Jesus did not need an expression of gratitude from the other nine, but He did know that for their growth as men, it was a trait they needed to learn and possess. One wonders if the cleansed Samaritan did not one day meet his nine colleagues and politely, but firmly, remind them that Jesus had inquired about them.

A genuine apology, a simple thank you, or a sincere expression of gratitude is almost always appreciated by the recipient of the apology and the giver of the gift. Christ, the Samaritan, and the nine who never turned back, teach each of us a simple, but important, lesson in human relationships.

An old lady in St. Petersburg, Russia, who had lost her pension after the collapse of the Soviet system, retaught me the lesson of the leper who returned to thank Christ for being healed. She ate one meal a day at a Salvation Army soup kitchen which had received considerable quantities of food from our Gulf War excesses. We were visiting the facility and toured the kitchen. The midday meal was about over when she figured out who we were and that I was the senior official in this strange group of Americans. She, of course, spoke no English and I spoke no Russian. That did not stop her from coming up to me and with a toothless smile and a weathered wrinkled face, giving me a big hug and profusely thanking me for the food donation. On that occasion I knew just a little how Christ felt when the single leper returned to express his gratitude.

The Blind Beggar with Great Courage

The Christian world is deeply indebted to the Apostle John for his account where Jesus heals a blind man on the Sabbath, and equally indebted to the man himself, for he was indeed a person, despite his low station in life, possessed of remarkable courage and strong character.

The ninth chapter of John carries within it numerous lessons regarding human conduct and a couple of brief doctrinal discourses by Jesus of great value to all disciples.

Unlike so many others healed by the Master, this man did not come seeking Jesus. Rather the Master saw him as He passed by the man somewhere in Jerusalem. Blind from birth, he was reduced to the profession of beggar to sustain himself. Upon seeing the man, His disciples asked Jesus a question frequently posed by the Jews. "Master, who did sin, this man, or his parents, that he was born blind?" (*John 9:2*).

Jesus' reply dispelled both aspects of the question. The man had been born blind, said the Savior, not because of his sins or those of his parents but that "the works of God should be manifest in him." *(John 9:3)* Little did this good and courageous man know that the light of day, the beauties of the earth, the face of his dear mother, and the grandeur of a sunset had been withheld from him for a divine and noble purpose. The darkness in his life was about to end and the precious gift of sight would come through the power and compassion of the incredible Man from Galilee.

Having established that He was the light of the world and sent to do "the works of him that sent me," Jesus then turned to this blind beggar and changed his life forever. *(John 9:4-7)*

Jesus used a most unique method to cure the man's blindness. After spitting on the ground, He made a wet clay which He applied to the man's eyes. No initial dialogue between Jesus and the man is recorded by John. However, we can almost certainly assume that Jesus talked to the man, perhaps asking his name and whether he wished to receive his sight. The beggar's characteristics of obedience, faith, and courage were certainly known to Jesus beforehand and would be reconfirmed most graphically as the man dealt with the hypocritical Pharisees who tried their best to entrap him and discredit Jesus.

After placing the moist clay on the man's eyes, Jesus then instructed him to go to the Pool of Siloam and wash. The man faithfully obeyed Christ's directive and as promised received his sight. Little did he know or understand at that moment how the Pharisees would deal with him, but he proved to be more than a match for those hypocrites. Christ's healing of this unfortunate blind man on the Sabbath became another gauntlet thrown down by the Master at the feet of His determined adversaries.

The restoration of the man's sight, like most of Christ's miracles, did not go unnoticed. Friends who had known him for years as a blind beggar wondered how his sight had been restored. Others questioned if it were really him, or perhaps this sighted man simply resembled the blind beggar. To him the question was posed.

> How were thine eyes opened?
>
> He answered and said, A man that is called Jesus made clay, and anointed mine eyes, and said unto me, Go to the pool of Siloam, and wash: and I went and washed, and I received sight.
>
> *John 9:10-11*

His questioners and doubters then took the man to the Pharisees who had learned that Jesus had performed this miracle on the Sabbath, a fact which intensified their hatred toward the Master. They showed no willingness to consider this miracle worker as a prophet, let alone the Son of God. They didn't have enough honesty and strength of character to regard the gift of sight as proof that Jesus possessed remarkable power. The Pharisees' spiritual blindness far exceeded this man's former physical blindness. As in all their dealings with Christ, they once again chose a course of disbelief, hatred, and cold-hearted opposition. They conspired to use this humble beggar to discredit the Man who had been so bold as to heal someone on the Sabbath.

John tells us that the man was brought to the Pharisees, but does not give us the venue where the man was questioned; a synagogue perhaps, maybe the temple, or perhaps the home of a leading member of that group. Suddenly the poor beggar who had plead for alms from those who passed his way, who almost certainly was unlettered and unlearned in religious law, found himself being questioned and cajoled by men of great learning and status in Jewish society. He would, or so they thought, be a push-over and certainly help them discredit this Galilean Jew who in their view had so blatantly violated the Jewish Sabbath. This remarkable and courageous man proved them wrong on every count. They did not know or understand that he had gained profound respect for Jesus, that he was very honest, and possessed under the ragged exterior of a blind beggar a sharp mind and —most of all— the courage to defend the truth as he had just experienced it.

Their opening attack on Jesus through the former blind man was two pronged. Some stated that "the man is not of God, because he keepeth not the Sabbath. Others said, How can a man that is a sinner do such miracles." *(John 9:16)*

Although their own minds were closed regarding Jesus, they did show the beggar the courtesy of asking his view of the Man who healed him. Without hesitation, he gave a clear and emphatic answer, "He is a prophet," words which they did not want to hear. *(John 9:17)*

The Pharisees quickly realized that they must pursue a different course, for the man obviously was not going to give the answers they so desperately wanted to hear from him. In their perverse minds, they reasoned that perhaps this man was never blind. If that could be proven, they could trap Jesus and the former blind man in a serious hoax.

In a desperate move they called into their presence the man's parents. That they were devout Jews is shown by their fear of what the Pharisees could do to them, especially banishment from the synagogue. When asked by the Pharisees if this man was indeed their son, if he had been born blind, and "how then doth he now see?", they answered both truthfully and evasively. *(John 9:19)*

> His parents answered them and said, We know that this is our son, and that he was born blind.
>
> But by what means he now seeth, we know not; or who hath opened his eyes, we know not: he is of age; ask him: he shall speak for himself.
>
> *John 9:20-21*

Their second answer was not a profile in courage. After truthfully acknowledging that he was indeed their son and that in fact he had been born blind, the parents were not willing to go any further. Although it is possible that their son never mentioned the name of Jesus to them, it is much more probable that he did. At some point they had learned of his great and miraculous gift of sight; human nature would seem to dictate that they would ask their son how he had been given his vision. It is equally fair and reasonable to assume that he told them, as he told others, that Jesus had performed the miracle. Whatever they knew or did not know, their answer will be judged by Christ alone.

The parents' testimony that he was their son and was indeed born blind was another defeat for the Pharisees, and forced them to once again deal with the former blind man direct. The dialogue that follows is, in the author's view, one of the most profound and courageous responses ever recorded in scripture. That it was spoken by a nameless, simple layman is even more impressive. His were words that spoke simple truths; he confronted hatred, bitterness and conspiracy, expressed sincere appreciation for the gift of a precious miracle, and uttered a simple, but genuine confession of discipleship.

> Then again called they the man that was blind, and said unto him, Give God the praise: we know that this man is a sinner.
>
> He answered and said, Whether he be a sinner or no, I know not: one thing I know, that, whereas I was blind, now I see.
>
> Then said they to him again, What did he to thee? how opened he thine eyes?
>
> He answered them, I have told you already, and ye did not hear: wherefore would ye hear it again? will ye also be his disciples?
>
> Then they reviled him, and said, Thou art his disciple; but we are Moses' disciples.
>
> We know that God spake unto Moses: as for this fellow, we know not from whence he is.
>
> The man answered and said unto them, Why herein is a marvelous thing, that ye know not from whence he is, and yet he hath opened mine eyes.
>
> Now we know that God heareth not sinners: but if any man be a worshipper of God, and doeth his will, him he heareth.
>
> Since the world began was it not heard that any man opened the eyes of one that was born blind.

> If this man were not of God, he could do nothing.
>
> They answered and said unto him, Thou wast altogether born in sins, and dost thou teach us? And they cast him out.
>
> *John 9:24-34*

John tells us that Jesus became aware that the man had been cast out, not only from the venue where the Pharisees had so unsuccessfully cross examined him, but most probably from his local synagogue. The Master sought the man and when He had found him, posed the eternal question.

> Dost thou believe on the Son of God?
>
> He answered and said, Who is he, Lord, that I might believe on him?
>
> And Jesus said unto him, Thou hast both seen him, and it is he that talketh with thee.
>
> *John 9:35-37*

The Apostle author indicates that this was the first time the formerly blind beggar had "seen" the face of Christ. Earlier the Master's voice had resonated in his ears and left an eternal impression. He had defended Jesus before the Pharisees and rejected the false notion that he had received sight by any other means than through the Son of God.

Our last scriptural association with this simple but great and courageous man is recorded briefly. "And he said, Lord, I believe. And he worshipped him." (*John 9:38)*

The former blind beggar then fades into historical and scriptural obscurity, having left a legacy of remarkable faith, great courage, and simple eloquence. Like the others in this narrative, he proved once again that common men and women were deeply loved and respected by the Master, and frequently possessed uncommon courage, faith, and tenacity.

The Sub Saharan Drought

As noted earlier in this work, Christ told his disciples in Matthew 25:40 that "Inasmuch as ye have done it unto the least of these my brethren, ye have done it unto me." I do not question the existence and role of guardian and ministering angels in this world. Many people have documented angelic assistance in their lives. In the main however, the Lord Jesus Christ leaves that role to his mortal sons and daughters. During the nearly ten years I administered humanitarian programs for the US Government and the LDS Church I did not meet a single spiritual ministering angel. The task of doing "unto the least of these my brethren" [and sisters] was performed by American GIs, Catholic Priests, Salvation Army officers, dedicated social workers, faithful LDS humanitarian missionaries, and compassionate service sisters to name just a few of this charitable force who in their own way and own right are ministering angels for the world's sick, hungry, downtrodden, and lonely. So it was as my colleagues and I tackled one of the world's great humanitarian crises in Africa.

During a devastating African drought in the mid 1980's, which took so many lives and caused so much human misery, I was appointed as the Department of Defense representative on a U.S. Government delegation to the Sudan with the assignment to try and solve the serious breakdown in the delivery of humanitarian relief supplies to refugees in Western Sudan. What all humanitarian workers worldwide know, and few others understand, is that the transportation and delivery of relief supplies is often more difficult and critical than obtaining the food, clothing, or medicines themselves for victims of drought, disaster, and conflict.

Our first stop in trying to discover the breakdown in transportation to Sudan was in the capital, Khartoum, where the United Nations and the USAID warehouses were located. We found those warehouses bulging with sorghum, which is a food grain frequently used as a bulk source of food for refugees, and other relief supplies. Getting that food from Khartoum to a huge black communal cooking pot in the Western Sudan desert was the real challenge facing us. We next flew by helicopter to certain desert refugee camps in the course of our inspection, and we saw first hand why the Sudanese railroad was having such a difficult time delivering relief supplies. It needed an inordinate amount of maintenance work to repair track, bridges and rolling stock. It also did not have the funds to accomplish those tasks and we and the refugees did not have the time to wait any longer. Trucks alone could not move the necessary quantities. We quickly realized that delivery of the relief supplies from Khartoum to the camps was our first priority.

Our delegation visited one particular camp where most of the refugees were from Chad. What I saw that day further changed my life and my eternal perspective about God's children. There were hundreds of people in what can loosely be described as a camp. A few had brought some kind of cloth and had made small, but rickety makeshift tents. Outside of the camp were numerous mounds, some rock covered, with a small crooked stick marking them as a burial site for those who had died of starvation, disease, or dehydration. As we neared the camp, a mother carrying a small child approached us begging for food and water. The child in her arms was near death, having all of the external symptoms of starvation. Throughout the rest of my mortal life, I shall never forget the helplessness I felt that hour. We had brought no food because of the helicopter ride, but my mind went back to the warehouses in Khartoum that were bulging with rice and sorghum. The misery, hopelessness, and pain in her face was one of the most difficult experiences I had ever known. Humanitarian workers deal with these realities and emotions frequently, but for me it was tough, not unlike the hospital in Hue. As I looked into her face, I prayed silently that God would bless and save her and her child and the people in that wretched camp. Although I do not know for sure, I suspect that her child died shortly thereafter. In the immediate term, I knew they were in God's hands. I whispered, mostly to myself, that I could not understand, but I still knew that God loved and cared for her and her child, and that someday Christ's atonement and Gospel would be hers to know. That experience convinced me that in some way or another, I had to join that small cadre of humanitarian workers worldwide who could help fulfill Christ's mandate in Chapter 25 of Matthew.

If there was a happy ending to this tragedy which I observed, it occurred when we got back to Washington, DC. Lt. General Julius Becton, Jr., US Army Retired, the Director of the Office of Foreign Disaster Assistance in USAID, and I knew there was only one answer to the delivery crisis— we needed heavy lift helicopters in that region and we needed them fast. Over considerable objections from some members of what has been frequently and too accurately described as the faceless bureaucracy, we convinced the senior leadership in AID, State and DOD to pay the cost of using C-5 transport aircraft to fly heavy duty helicopters from the Northwestern United States to Khartoum. Within a few days after our return to Washington, DC., sorghum and other food grains were being delivered to refugee camps throughout Western Sudan. I always hoped that the helicopter deliveries saved the lives of that woman and her child. God knows, and someday I hope to get an answer.

Orphanages—Good and Bad

As difficult as my visit to Romanian orphanages, noted below, was to accept and understand, I had another experience in an orphanage in Somalia that had quite the opposite effect. The circumstances were very different. As poor as Somalia is, the government and the administrators of that particular orphanage treated their precious charges as worthwhile human beings. The assistance the United States and other governments were giving to Somalia during its period of anarchy in the early 1990's was very difficult to accomplish. Most of the private humanitarian organizations had found it necessary to stop making food deliveries because much of it was being stolen at gun point by common thugs and militiamen. Under such circumstances, the lives of international relief workers were seriously threatened. At great cost, the American Government deployed hundreds of battle equipped troops to deliver the food to the towns and villages where it was so badly needed.

It was during one of these deliveries that I visited the orphanage in Northern Somalia. The children were an absolute inspiration to me. Despite the shortage of food in the area, they were reasonably well fed and their clothes were clean and neat. The biggest surprise and the most touching thing that happened during the visit was their music. Although I'm sure it was planned and pre-arranged, the children began singing as our group walked through the door. Their faces radiated and their smiles were infectious and genuine. When they finished singing, they gathered around us and told us their names as they laughed and giggled. With no parents to love them and no place to call home, they were still at least on that day happy, bubbly, and certainly always children of God. The impact on me was as positive as was the Romanian visit negative. Seldom had I seen such bubbling happiness among God's children who had so little.

Those wonderful Somalian orphans did not fully eliminate my attachment to natural comforts, but they surely made me appreciate what I had and taught me anew that the spirit of a child is indeed divine. These remarkable kids proved again that one of man's purposes in this life is to be joyful.

The plight of Romania's orphans in Ceaucescu's Romania has been well documented by the world media. ("Romania's Lost Children: A Photo Essay by James Nachtwey," New York Times, 24 June 1990) It was indeed one of the true horror stories of the last years of the 20th Century. The condition and treatment of these precious children were received in horror by caring people the world over. In most cases, they were treated like animals and warehoused like cattle. Response to their plight brought a great deal of help and relief. As tough as the hospital and burn center was in Hue, and the desert camp in Sudan, my visit to one of these orphanages in Bucharest was even more difficult to understand and accept. Those children were as badly treated as it was possible to treat children without physically beating them to death. Their spirits were numb, their personalities had been destroyed, and the sparkling eyes and impish smiles so common to children everywhere were absent. Warfare and atrocities, with all of their evil and inhumane treatment, are in most cases inflicted by adults upon adults. The Romanian orphans were in fact victims of inhumane treatment inflicted by a very brutal Communist regime. Seldom in recent history has a class of helpless human beings been more evilly and inhumanely treated. It was the closest I ever came to looking Satan straight in the eye.

Over the years there have been countless people who have left indelible impressions on my mind. These people, representing only a very small percentage of the victims worldwide, were, I believe, deeply loved by Christ. Each needed a caregiver and a helping hand from someone.

Thousands of refugees in a camp in Northeastern Ethiopia, where the roof over their head was a piece of tin or cardboard or a battered piece of canvas, tugged at my heartstrings. Their food was a gruel made from sorghum and sometimes other grains which were cooked in large black pots over an open fire. Toilet facilities and sanitation were much more rudimentary than an old American outhouse.

In distributing the 1,450 sea containers of food, which were transferred to me for the Department of Defense Humanitarian Program, we made an offer to the Government of Albania, which gladly accepted it. We flew a C-141 into Tirana with thirteen Air Force cargo pallets of food, and upon arrival at the airport I was asked if I and other members of my group would like to go meet Mother Teresa in her headquarters. I knew she did most of her work in India and South Asia, but did not know that she was Albanian and headquartered in Tirana. We had a short but inspirational meeting, and then she inquired if she could receive some of the food aboard the C-141 for her orphanages in Tirana. We of course could not refuse her request. Shortly thereafter, she arrived at the airbase in a jeep and we proceeded to offload as many boxes of food as that holy little vehicle would hold. Before she left, she went on board the aircraft, thanked the crew, and blessed the mission. Now for the rest of the story.

If my measuring skills were accurate, I believe that Mother Teresa was not more than five feet tall and physically very small in stature. In that little lady, however, was a very powerful, loving, and determined spirit. Her care for the poor had become legendary, and after visiting and talking with her for a short time I came to know why. It was a cherished moment in my life to meet someone who was "...doing it unto the least of these my brethren."

CHAPTER EIGHT

CHRIST'S ATONEMENT AND HIS GOSPEL OF JOY

All that has been written in this small treatise is subsumed in the atoning sacrifice of Jesus Christ. God the Father ordained it, Christ committed to accomplish it, and the Old Testament and Book of Mormon prophets assured mankind that it would come to pass in the meridian of time. The Gospel writers and the ancient apostles, except Judas, gave powerful witnesses that it happened just as Christ said it would throughout His brief earthly ministry. In 3 Nephi 10-18 in the Book of Mormon, a second powerful witness was written by men who knew, saw, and touched the wounds of the resurrected Christ in America. This divine book of scripture was given to the world in 1830 by Joseph Smith, who also saw and spoke personally with God the Father and the Resurrected Christ.

The prophetic witnesses from Adam to our modern prophets are there for the world to accept or reject. After all the witnesses and scripture are considered, acceptance of Christ as the Savior of mankind is something which each person must decide. It cannot be evaded or placed on another's shoulders.

In closing this brief work which describes the Jesus I know, it is appropriate to put on record my own convictions and witness of Christ as the Redeemer of all mankind and as my personal Savior.

My first reason is logic and reasoning. This pillar of my testimony is heresy to some people in the LDS Church, who believe that the only way to gain a testimony of Christ is through the Holy Ghost. I completely agree that it is through the Holy Ghost that the witnessing conviction must come, but let me make my case for a role for knowledge and reason in gaining a firm witness of Christ's divinity. Mormon missionaries from 1830 until now have frequently heard from an investigator something similar to these words: " If God spoke to the ancients, it is only logical that He will speak to us." Others after having the creation of man explained to them say, "I have always believed that when Genesis says we were created in the image of God, that God was a person with a body like us." "If Christ organized a Church in Jerusalem with twelve apostles, any Church claiming to be Christ's Church must also have apostles."

Logic and reason serve other purposes. That there is some evolution in nature seems to me to be irrefutable. Conversely, it is patently ridiculous to assume that man came from a blob or mass millions of years ago. Man is too marvelous a creature to have been a mistake or a chance. His intellect and the power of pro-creation simply attest that man and woman truly are creations of a loving God.

The order in the universe bears a dramatic witness of the existence of God. The face of a child, the beauty of the earth, and the exquisiteness of the seasons all testify of a living Deity. The maturing of a great oak tree from a single acorn lends reason to God's hand in the creation of man and the earth.

Standing at the open grave of a precious child, a beloved spouse, or a wonderful mother, reason and logic send a clear and unmistaken message that death is not the end.

Am I a nobody, created only by a sexual act which ends forever when the last breath escapes my lips? Were my thoughts, dreams, hopes, love, family associations, successes, and struggles but a temporary blip on the screen of eternity destined to disappear forever? That conclusion "makes reason stare," to this question of man's divinity, if I may apply Eliza R. Snow's line from her great hymn, "O My Father."

Some years ago, I was flying home to Virginia from Rhein Main AFB in Germany on an Air Force C-5. The pilots sometimes allowed me to ride in the huge cockpit which had extra seats for crew or observers. On this night I was privileged to see the Northern Lights in all of their grandeur. Astronauts have similarly noted the spectacular nature of mother earth and the order in space.

An accident? No divine power behind it all?! Man is a blob without a divine spark and identity? Something in my mind whispers that such conclusions are nonsense!

I turn next to the Restored Gospel and Church. No one can deny that the Church has faced many problems since its inception. The Gospel is perfect; the Church has a way to go. Mistakes and failures in the Church have been numerous, ranging from Joseph Smith's establishment of a banking system in Kirtland that failed miserably to the aborted eighteen-month mission adopted by the Church in the early 1980's. Such problems, are in my opinion, a witness of the divinity of this latter-day work. The Lord runs the Church through human beings. He lets them "study it out in your own minds." *(D&C 9:7-9)* Church leaders at all levels do not always get it right the first time. These factors have sometimes been the basis of apostasy by some members of the Church, but for me these things have strengthened my faith and convictions. I read of Mormon and Moroni's expressions of inadequacies, of Peter's progress from an unlettered fisherman to Chief Apostle and the benefactor of Tabitha. The candor and honesty of Church leaders in telling us that they work hard and sometimes struggle as they administer the Church is appreciated and refreshing to me and most Latter-day Saints.

As President Gordon B. Hinckley stated in the Priesthood Sessionof General Conference, April 1995: "Now in the ongoing of this work, administrative changes sometimes occur. The doctrine remains constant. But from time to time there are organizational and administrative changes made under provisions set forth in the revelations."

In October 2013 President Dieter F. Uchtdorf stated in the Saturday Morning Session of General Conference:

"Some struggle with unanswered questions about things that have been done or said in the past. We openly acknowledge that in nearly 200 years of Church history—along with an uninterrupted line of inspired, honorable, and divine events—there have been some things said and done that could cause people to question. Sometimes questions arise because we simply don't have all the information and we just need a bit more patience. When the entire truth is eventually known, things that didn't make sense to us before will be resolved to our satisfaction. Sometimes there is a difference of opinion as to what the "facts" really mean. A question that creates doubt in some can, after careful investigation, build faith in others. And, to be perfectly frank, there have been times when members or leaders in the Church have simply made mistakes. There may have been things said or done that were not in harmony with our values, principles, or doctrine.

I suppose the Church would be perfect only if it were run by perfect beings. God is perfect, and His doctrine is pure. But He works through us—His imperfect children—and imperfect people make mistakes."

My final argument in support of reason and logic playing a useful role in one's testimony is this: the LDS Church is now over 180 years old. Its growth and power as a religion in the world is reaching unprecedented proportions. If it were a Church of a man, with all of its incredible doctrines and teachings, it would have collapsed a long time ago. The death of Joseph Smith, the practice of plural marriage, and the exodus from Nauvoo to the Great Basin would have killed any organization but Christ's Restored Church. What then has carried the Church for these past eighteen decades? Christ at the helm is the major reason. Prophets, revelation, latter-day scripture, temples and the missionary program have played important and significant roles. Without the faith and testimonies, however, of its individual members, the Church could not survive. These are people who know that this Gospel is true and this is Christ's Church. This conviction causes them to serve, attend Church meetings (some of which are very mediocre), pay tithing, go on missions, sustain Church leadership at all levels, and build the Kingdom in grateful anticipation of Christ's return to the earth. The most critical element of this witness is the knowledge that Jesus, as the Son of God, atoned for our sins and arose from the grave nearly 2,000 years ago.

May I record now my own appreciation and interpretation of the last three days of Christ's life. My focus will be limited to the Savior's agony in Gethsemane, certain aspects of his trial before the Jewish and Roman authorities, and his actual crucifixion and resurrection.

Recently my wife and I and other dear family members visited the Holy Land, including the Garden of Gethsemane. I was deeply touched again by the fact that Christ plead three times to His Father to be relieved of the burden of the atonement, only to be told that the cup could and would not be removed. God's decision was more than a simple "no" to his Beloved Son. It was the greatest expression of love for me, my loved ones, and all of mankind that was ever expressed by the God of Heaven. To paraphrase John's quote in Chapter 3, verse 16: "For God so loved the world that He told his Beloved Son 'No' three times."

Christ's trial, of course, has been well documented. However, there is one aspect thereof which most of us miss. We have vilified the Jewish Sanhedrin, Pilate, Herod, and the Roman soldiers for their respective roles in Christ's death. The fact of the matter is their roles were necessary. The Jewish leaders demand for His crucifixion fulfilled numerous Old Testament prophesies. Under Roman law, however, they could neither pass sentence nor carry out His execution. Was Christ to go up to Calvary and nail himself on the cross? Of course not. Pilate, despite his finding no guilt in Christ, and following Herod's refusal to take jurisdiction in the case was the only governing authority with the power to order Christ's death. And so he did order certain soldiers of the Roman garrison to carry out the execution, an act which Christ's Father had decreed must occur. The Sanhedrin, Pilate, and the Roman soldiers did what was necessary for Christ to carry out the atonement for all mankind.

The last living moments Christ spent on the cross were terribly painful for Him and His Father. As the Son of God approached death, His Father performed another necessary and painful act. Perhaps even more difficult than Gethsemane, Elohim withdrew His support, power, and influence from Christ, thus requiring Him to accomplish the final act of the atonement entirely alone. While I can understand the need for that withdrawal, I cannot comprehend the painful agony for both the Father and Son to do so. The Father's agony we can only assume; Christ's is recorded in Chapter 27 of Matthew "Eli Eli Lama Sabachthani," that is to say "My God, my God why hast thou forsaken me?" In Christ's entire life and atonement mission, nothing had been more profoundly difficult. He recovered quickly and in a bold voice reestablished the bond with His God, "Father, into Thy hands I commend my spirit." The atonement of Christ was then completed. Some 36 hours later, having visited the Spirit World, Christ rose triumphantly from the borrowed tomb where he had been placed after His death. Mary Magdalene, for reasons known only to Christ and perhaps herself, became the first mortal to see and witness Christ's victory over death. *(John 20:11-18)* Her short dialogue with the angel describes the most important scripture ever recorded in the history of mankind. Matthew records it as follows. Speaking to the women the angel said, "Fear not ye: for I know that ye seek Jesus, which was crucified. He is not here: for he is [a]risen, as he said." (Matt 28: 5-6)

In Gethsemane, Christ took the sins of the world upon himself, mine included. On Calvary, he made the sacrifice required by His Father in the Councils of Heaven. By walking out of the tomb, He won the victory over death and gave to all mankind the gift of immortality, and eternal life to those who would choose to earn it.

This is the Jesus I know: a dear friend and my personal Savior.

I turn now to the principle pillar of my own convictions and witness. To most of the outside world, things of the Spirit are strange to say the least. Things of the Spirit in the LDS Church are stranger still.

In closing this book I express the following testimony and convictions.

I deeply appreciate the divine guidance provided through the scriptures, prayer, and prophetic guidance. They are critical anchors and pillars in my faith and the teachings of Christ and His restored gospel. It is not easy to explain, but somehow the Spirit whispers to my mind that this is all true. Such an experience with the Holy Ghost can be told, but not always explained; one must experience it to understand it. The uniqueness and greatness of this witness according to Christ,

Peter, Moroni, Joseph Smith and every humble missionary who has, is now, or will serve as an emissary of Christ, is available to any man or woman who will honestly and prayerfully seek it. God is no respecter of persons. All mankind is eligible for the divine gift. *(Moroni 10:4-6)*

One of the most reassuring aspects of my religious convictions is that God and Christ are perfectly fair. From Adam until now, there have been gross injustices in the world. In the final judgment, the Jesus I know will correct whatever needs correcting. Of this I am surely convinced. The system of divine justice, administered by Christ and His subordinate judges, will be perfectly fair and right. Everything in a person's life will be properly and correctly weighed and considered, and when the judgment is rendered, each one of us will certainly know that it is fair and just. As noted in the first pages of this book, no one will be given something they did not earn or deserve, and unlike this life, no one will be deprived of what is rightfully theirs.

This is a Gospel of joy! As we go through life struggling to endure to the end, making ourselves more Christ-like, and listening to the unending and constant reminders from the pulpit to repent, serve and be better people, we sometimes lose sight of the fact that Christ's burdens and yoke are light and that "men are, that they might have joy." *(2 Nephi 2:25)* We could use a little more humor in the Church and a lot less guilt. I suggest three remedies: 1) read the Gospel writers' accounts of Christ's resurrection, 2) recall frequently your great love and physical intimacy with your sweetheart, and 3) look into the face of a precious, happy child.

I have come to believe that sooner or later it will come down to my wife and me. While our children are sealed to us and we to our parents as eternal families, the Lord has told us in the 76th and 132nd Sections of the Doctrine and Covenants, and in the temple, that it is husband and wife who qualify for exaltation, perfection, and eventually Godhood. Such is the divine plan. It started with our first date, the welcome onset of romance, and a six month courtship. It was crowned at the altar in the Logan Utah Temple, and despite some bumps and challenges along the way, it has turned into one great eternal love.

To my readers, my children and their families, and certain friends, I say that my greatest possession is my beautiful, sexy and wonderful wife. My marriage to her is the highlight of my mortal and eternal existence. Spending eternity with her is my greatest ambition and blessing.

The Jesus I know is the author of this great union and indescribable blessing.

The Jesus I know is a dear friend and confidant. He loves me and my sweetheart and family with a divine love that is endless and perhaps not yet fully appreciated. He created the earth and was born in Bethlehem just as the scriptures say. His ministry in the Holy Land, in America, and among the lost tribes was focused on bringing love and joy to anyone who would be a disciple. I close with my witness that He rose triumphant from the grave, thereby giving to me the gift of eternal life, if I am worthy.

I look forward to someday meeting, embracing, and thanking the Jesus I know.

CPSIA information can be obtained at www.ICGtesting.com
Printed in the USA
BVOW11s1104191215

430480BV00028B/369/P